MW00775428

ADVANCE REVIEWS

"FAIRYTALE is not only a fascinating show business story, but also a look at the journey of one of America's top pop singing group's... it's a history lesson in perseverance, ambition, and the joy of performing. Anita was my high school classmate and although we were friends and shared the stage at Oakland Technical High School, I was truly in the dark of her journey as a talent."

TED LANGE, Actor, Director, and Screenwriter

"A compassionate, hilarious, smart, transparent and engaging family history. FAIRYTALE is a must-read, an extraordinary account of an African American family's resilience and perpetual evolution."

DR. EVELYN REID, Professor, Social Justice Education

"With incredible grace, beauty, and insight, Anita and Fritz Pointer bring to life an endearing family story, which is part of the complex arc of the American Dream and the dream deferred. This wonderful book captures the story of striving beyond all odds to reach what could only be understood as mythological heights, during times of deep racial segregation and discrimination, to create a worldwide musical sensation, spanning four decades. The authors fearlessly address the pain and sacrifices along the way, giving readers a searing, vulnerable account of an American fairytale. You will cheer their successes, weep for personal losses, and not want to put the book down."

MICHELE BRATCHER GOODWIN, Chancellor's Professor
Director, Center for Biotechnology & Global Health Policy
University of California, Irvine School of Law, Author of
*Black Markets: The Supply and Demand of Body Parts; Baby Markets:
Money* and *The New Politics of Creating Families*

"Anita and brother Fritz Pointer have combined their wisdom to deliver us a vivid an intriguing story on how an Oakland Bay Area family, raised by Church of God ministers, become international pop superstars. The Pointer Sisters are an inspiration to us all, especially those of us who love music and understand how important it is to the world."

DR. TERENCE ELLIOTT, Professor of Popular Music: Rock,
Rhythm & Blues, and Hip Hop, Author of *Spirit, Rhythm, and
Story: Community Building and Healing through Song*

"As I read FAIRYTALE, I was drawn into many worlds; the worlds of Jim Crow America, adversity, family support and stubbornly strong personal identities; all tied to their passion for music and harmony and creating the background soundtrack of the Sisters' story. The world of their music, always developing and changing form and shape with them, is a complex and driving force in Fritz and Anita's fearlessly intimate and warm narrative of their family's life. We have been blessed with the Pointer Sisters' music. I heartily recommend that you listen to it again while reading this book. It'll transport you into another world."

DR. RALPH KNUDSON

"The extraordinary accomplishments of the Pointer Sisters and the family story go well beyond reaching the peak summits of the music business documented here in rich detail. Their namesake derives from the Pointer plantation in Virginia during slavery. Despite these 'lowly' origins, every member of the modern Pointer clan has achieved unusually high levels of career success. A strong loving family tradition competes with the individual personal needs and egos of these highly talented sisters who face the opportunities and temptations that come with Hollywood fame and fortune."

DR. ROGER KOTILA, Psychologist, Peace Activist, President of Democratic World Federalists based in San Francisco

"The searing painful and uplifting story that Anita and Fritz Pointer share of the Pointer family...is an enthralling, heartbreaking and still, inspiring tale. Battling through racism, addiction, the loss of parents, a brilliant sister, and ultimately a beautiful daughter.

FAIRYTALE deserves to be taken very seriously. It belongs in every university, library, and home. To comprehend the depth of this very important and scholarly work requires maturity and a realization of music, complex adult relationships, and, ultimately, survival... despite tremendous pain. Anita and her family grew up in the church, and there is no doubt that the Hand of God is with this family through each hurt, discrimination, mistake, and triumph. Congratulations, Anita. I've always loved you... and now, I truly know you."

KATHY IRELAND, Author, Actor, Entrepreneur, Model

FAIRYTALE

FAIRYTALE
The Pointer Sisters'
FAMILY STORY

ANITA POINTER <u>AND</u> FRITZ POINTER

WITH
DAVE SMITHERMAN

Wyatt-MacKenzie Publishing
DEADWOOD, OREGON

Fairytale: The Pointer Sisters' Family Story

Anita Pointer and Fritz Pointer

with Dave Smitherman

ISBN: 978-1-948018-38-8 Hardcover Library Edition

ISBN: 978-1-948018-39-5 Trade Paperback

Library of Congress Control Number: 2020930279

Wyatt-MacKenzie Publishing
DEADWOOD, OREGON

Wyatt-MacKenzie Publishing, Inc., Deadwood, OR

www.wyattmackenzie.com (541) 964-3314

Requests for permission or further information should be addressed to: Wyatt-MacKenzie Publishing, 15115 Highway 36, Deadwood, Oregon 97430

CONTENTS

DEDICATION

This book is dedicated to all the folks who inspired and helped us but joined the ancestors before they could see the fruits of our labor, especially...Herman, and Frankie Pointer (fraternal grandparents), Eva Pointer (fraternal aunt), Elton and Sarah Pointer (parents), June Pointer (sister), Jada (Harper) Pointer (Anita's daughter), Fritz and Roxie Silas (maternal grandparents), Horace Silas (maternal uncle), Leon Sr. and Clara Mae Silas (maternal uncle and aunt), William "Pie" Silas (maternal cousin), Leon Silas, Jr. (maternal cousin), David Mudavanha Patterson (friend and advisor), Ray and Inez (East) Dones (Leona's parents), Daniel and Selina Kunene (Liziwe's parents).

ACKNOWLEDGEMENT/

This book could not have been written without the knowledge, assistance, and encouragement of: the Pointer family for believing in us; The West Oakland Church of God, the Watson Sisters, Ephesians Church of God in Christ (Andrae Crouch and Billy Preston), DeFremery Park (mentors: Dorothy Pitts, Ruth Beckford, Bill Patterson, Ernest Howard), Miss Gellett (Music Teacher, Westlake Jr. High), Mr. Whayne (Drama Teacher, Oakland Technical HS), Mr. Mullins (Band Teacher McRae HS, Prescott, Arkansas), Ms. Hill (English Teacher, McClymonds HS), David Rubinson, Bill Graham, Bruce Good, Jeffery Cohen, Elvin Bishop, Taj Mahal, Bonnie Raitt, Grace Slick, Dave Mason, Sylvester, The Cockettes, Forest Hamilton, Jerry Weintraub, Sandy Gallin, Jim Morey, Ben Bernstein, Steve Levine, Gibson & Stromberg, Debbie Shine, Marc Vogel, Jervonny Collier, Norman Landsberg, Nathan East, Tom Salisbury, Stevie Wonder, Bruce Springsteen, Bruce Willis, Whoopi Goldberg, Sterling Winters Company and Kathy Ireland Worldwide, Richard and Roger Perry, Paul Ciulla, Dr. Evelyn Reid, Odelia Gonzelis, Carol Lamere, Azure McCall, Rita Minor, Paula Stewart, Gwen Davis, Jeanne Ricks, Amelia Patterson, Mary Kay, Laurel Fead, Debbie Landers, Gina Glasscock, Gina Harper, Cecille Parker, Seri Culpepper, Trevor Lawrence, Tom Snow, Allee Willis, Sheldon Reynolds, Flip Wilson, Carol Burnett, Dick Clark, Ralph Johnson, Don Mischer (Producer: *Pointer Sisters' Up All Night Special*), Leonard Feather, Bob Krasnow (Blue Thumb Records), Dr. Ralph and Nancy Knudson, Lynn Roman, Shirley Gonzales, Pat Blake, Brenda Lacy, Jimmy Hildreth, Teri and Steve Diamond, Preston and Gina Glass, and Congresswoman Maxine Waters, and our book team: William Briggs, Todd Shuster, Konrad Leh, Michael Prochelo, Leslie Komaru, Laura Hanifin and our friend and publisher Nancy Cleary.

One-Way Ticket
by Langston Hughes

I pick up my life

And take it on the train

To Los Angeles, Bakersfield, Seattle, Oakland, Salt Lake,
Any place that is
North and West – And not South.

I am fed up

With Jim Crow laws, People who are cruel And afraid,
Who lynch and run, Who are scared of me And me of them.

I pick up my life And take it away
On a one-way ticket – Gone up North,
Gone out West, Gone!

Chapter 1

EVER AFTER

BEING IN THE HIT MUSIC GROUP THE POINTER SISTERS FOR FIVE decades has been an amazing roller coaster ride through the world of music and stardom. Like any group, we had our ups and downs, but when I first saw my sisters Bonnie and June perform, I decided right then and there to quit my 9-to-5 at a law firm. Even though I enjoyed answering calls, filing papers, and greeting clients, I wanted something different. I wanted to be on stage.

It was the best decision I've ever made, and I wouldn't trade that experience for anything. We were thrust into the dizzying world of show business with no professional training other than singing in the choir at our father's church, The West Oakland Church of God. Not only that, we knew nothing about royalties, songwriting credits, or management fees. The only thing we were sure of was that we loved singing and performing together. We were damn good at it right from the start, and we just kept getting better and better. As a result, the hits started coming.

You've seen those TV shows about people who literally get buried under their possessions and require an intervention to clean up their home and their life. Well, I don't think I'm a hoarder by definition, but I do love to collect things that are important to me and I always have. Somehow, throughout our whirlwind musical journey, I managed to amass a lot of amazing memorabilia. I'm not sure how I was able to hang onto so many dresses, scripts, lyrics, and autographs, but I did.

Whether we were headlining a concert, shooting a music video, or guest starring on *The Carol Burnett Show*, I would keep the outfit, jewelry, or some other items that I thought were important. It makes me sick to think of the things that I didn't get or the things I saved that were either lost or taken, but I can't dwell on that. I prefer to focus on the things that I do have, because they are a part of our history, of *my* history.

This habit of collecting has meant that I've become something of an expert on the workings of storage facilities. I can tell you the various sizes that are offered and help you with those confusing contracts. I've rented, filled, and unfilled many of them over the years. They are the key to maintaining a great collection while still managing to keep my home livable. Of course, I have some of my possessions at my house, but not too many. I don't plan to be featured on one of those TV shows. I can see the tabloid headline now: "The Pointer Sisters' Anita Pointer found buried under a pile of sequin dresses and wigs!"

No, I'm not going out like that, because I found something much better. Donelle Dadigan, Founder and President of the world-famous Hollywood Museum, gave me the opportunity to create an exhibit showcasing "50 years of Iconic Fashion, Wardrobe Design, and Memorabilia, created by the sensational career of The Pointer Sisters." It's the perfect way for me to share those historic items with the world and allow others to get as much joy from them as I do. They gave me the entire second floor of the museum, which is located in the Historic Max Factor Building on Hollywood and Highland in Los Angeles, and I filled it up!

Donelle said, "We are just so thrilled to have been chosen to display this incredible collection at The Hollywood Museum and present it to the public. I've been a fan of The Pointer Sisters for years. We have a very exciting and fun presentation planned out for this unique experience...we are not holding anything back!"

Thankfully I had the help of my granddaughter Roxie McKain, who acted as Project Manager, along with Creative Director Melissa Simpson. It took us over two years to decide what to display and how to catalog everything. Then we got to actually bring the exhibit to life with live videos, posters, jewelry, vintage merchandise, and even a disco floor!

We ended up with over 100 display items and named the show "Ever After" with the goal of educating museum visitors about not just the music industry, but also its influence on our country's political history. It covers the golden years of music and represents the many genres that The Pointer Sisters are known for: pop, disco, jazz, R&B, soul, funk, dance, and even country.

It is truly a passion project and one I'd thought about for a long time, but that process led to something even more amazing. Revisiting all the memories—the good and the bad—helped convince me that this is the perfect time to write my own story. With some help from my talented brother, Fritz, and feedback from the rest of the family, I was convinced that my time had come. Being part of the group was amazing and my sisters mean everything to me, but we all have our own journey and our own stories. Sure, we have the common thread of The Pointer Sisters that will always tie us together, but we've all been involved in creative projects of our own, like the "Ever After" exhibit I did at the Hollywood Museum.

When I hopped on stage with my sisters for the first time, I had no idea of the path my life would take, the people I would meet, and the things I would accomplish. I've been able to entertain and perform with my family and also enjoy my own successes like writing hit songs and recording a solo album. Naturally, not everything turned out exactly like I had hoped, but that's part of the journey. One of the most important lessons I've learned is to enjoy the process and stay in the moment. It's not the hits or misses that are most important. It's the experience I've had, the lives I've touched, and the memories I've made.

Chapter 2
HOTZIGADY

O UR DAD, ELTON POINTER, WAS BORN IN LITTLE ROCK, ARKANSAS in 1901. During the "Roaring Twenties," he was living in Chicago, Illinois and married to a woman named Susie. We don't know anything about her or even what happened to her. Dad certainly never talked about her, or the child they may or may not have had. In fact, he didn't talk much about his life back then. The very little he said was only to demonstrate the need, the necessity, for salvation. What we have pieced together is that his life of bootlegging, boosting, and what-have-you came to an abrupt halt when his partner in crime, wearing an overcoat Daddy had lent him, was shot in the back and killed. This epiphany, in 1936, demanded salvation, and Daddy "got saved." Not only did he get saved, he became a preacher.

Our mother, the only daughter among Grandma Roxie's and Granddaddy Fritz's five children, Sarah Elizabeth Silas, was born in Roseboro, Arkansas on January 13, 1924. She says that she was "about three pounds at birth...so small that men's handkerchiefs were used as diapers. They even carried me around on a pillow. I was so tiny Mother and Daddy didn't think I would live."

This, undoubtedly, accounts for the fact that Mother has a "De-layed Birth Certificate," from the Arkansas Bureau of Vital Statistics. Granddaddy Fritz and Grandma Roxie even took her around to see all the local relatives because they didn't think she would live too long. "A neighbor, a white woman," as Mother puts it, "Mrs. Boham, told Grandma Roxie to try fresh buttermilk. She did, and I've been getting fat ever since. My mother's milk had dried up after my birth, and Mrs. Boham would bring her fresh buttermilk for me every day... and every time I'd say, 'look Mommy, here come the lady with the titty milk.'" Grandma Roxie, her mother (who we called Grandma

Stevens), Granddaddy Fritz, the rest of the Silas clan, and the white neighbors all helped nurse little Sarah to health.

Grandma Roxie took her to church regularly. Granddaddy Fritz went sometimes. Mother loved the music, the preaching, and the singing—with or without a piano, a cappella. As a little girl, she liked to gather around her brothers—Fritz Jr., Leon, and Jack—and practice her preaching skills. While attending McRae Middle School, she joined a quartet that sang at various churches and camp meetings around Arkansas.

Because schools for African Americans stopped at the eighth grade, in 1937 at the age of 13, to further her education, her parents sent her to New York City to live with her aunt, Mrs. Addie Lockhart and her husband, William Lockhart. "At 234 Brad Hurst Avenue, apartment #232, up in Harlem," she said with noticeable pride. Addie Lockhart is Granddaddy Fritz's sister. She had no children of her own. Mother stayed in New York for two and a half years. Along with her cousin, Gustava Silas, she attended Washington Irving All Girls High School in the Bronx. She and Gustava lived with the Lockharts and were two of the three "colored" girls to attend the school. Truancy was closely watched in New York City, so Mother and Gustava would ride streetcars to school every day to make sure they arrived on time.

They took typical courses like English, Mathematics, Home Economics, Dietetics, American History, and Physical Education. Mother studied and prepared to be a dietitian. But, unimaginable to us, she was also a pitcher on the softball team, once even pitching a no-hitter. We couldn't imagine our mother, who we never saw in pants and tennis shoes, in a softball uniform. Sometimes it's hard for children to imagine their own parents as young people.

Apparently, Grandma Roxie asked Mother to return to Arkansas and told her, "There's this man I think you should marry. He's a preacher. He's nice-looking." So, it was at a camp meeting in Hope, Arkansas that Sarah met our father, Elton.

The marriage license from the State of Arkansas, in the county of Nevada, has at the top a handwritten note by Granddaddy Fritz stating: "This is to certify that I am willing for my daughter, Sarah Silas, to marry Elton Pointer...Father – Fritz Silas. This, no doubt, is because at the time our dad is listed as "aged 40" and our mother as "aged 17." They were married on July 19, 1941 in Little Rock. Once asked if she loved him, Mother said, "Can't say that I did. All I knew was that he was a 'saved' man, a good man, a man who would not raise his voice or his hand to me. A man I could learn to love." And in their 39 years of marriage, he never raised his voice to her, never raised his hand to her, and they were rarely apart. Once asked about this twenty-three-year age difference, she said, "I'd rather be an old man's lover than a young man's slave."

Our parents left Arkansas in 1945. They were part of the exodus, the six-decade-long "Great Migration" of almost six million black citizens of the United States who *fled* the South for northern and western cities in search of a better life. The operative word here is "fled." For, like most who left the land of their forefathers for an uncertain existence in almost every other corner of America, our parents were not only "migrants," they were also considered "refugees," fleeing the terror of the Jim Crow south.

Granddaddy Fritz deeply loved Sarah, his gorgeous daughter, our mother, and knowing the threat she faced during the tumultuous Civil Rights era, especially in the South, often said: "I was going to be killed or kill somebody." So, the family "packed up all their things and walked." Actually, they rode away, by car, ending up in California. Our clan, the Pointers and Silases, moved to Oakland for a better life.

Their first child, Aaron Elton, was born in Little Rock, Arkansas in 1942 and Fritz Herman came along a year later. Soon it was time for the girls. First there was Ruth Esther in 1946, I came along in 1948 and was named Anita Marie. Unlike the others, I was born in our family house, across the street from DeFremery Park, at 1176 18th Street—for fun, I called it "Lemdy Semdy," at 18th and Adeline. I used to think that me being born at home was an accident, that mother couldn't get to the hospital in time, that I had come early; but she told me that she had planned to have me at home; that she had a midwife and doctor there. Her best friend, Sister Lee, was there; and, of course there were Aaron and Fritz mischievously trying to peek through a keyhole to see as much as they could. Being the only one born at home did make me feel special.

Then there was Patricia Eva "Bonnie" in 1950 and finally June Antoinette in 1953. All us girls were born in Oakland, California. Mother said to us more than once that she "loved having children" and that it was the joy of her life. "Nothing" she said, "made me happier than having a baby. I thought it was one of the most wonderful miracles in life." And she loved us unconditionally. We could sit around the kitchen table with her until late into the night talking about anything and everything. Most of the time the topic was family: who's where, who's doing what, who's doing how, who's due when.

The exact date when The West Oakland Church of God began operation is not known. Earliest available records put the date sometime around early 1943. Founding Father, Elder Joe Eddens and Sister Emily, his wife, began holding meetings in their home at 945 Campbell Street. Soon, the little congregation moved its meeting place to a storefront location at 1699 8th Street.

In 1944, when his eyesight began to fail, Pastor Eddens resigned. Elder Moses E. Scott of Hanford, California, took up leadership of the congregation and pastored for a year, when he, too, resigned because of failing health. The congregation then called on our father, Elton Pointer, and he began leadership in June of 1945.

During Dad's first years, meeting places were not stable, but he and Mom and a committed group maintained a faith that was steadfast and unshakeable. They worshipped at the 8th Street storefront until early 1947 when the lease expired and could not be renewed. So, for a brief period they worshipped at 1002 Filbert Street, the home of Sister Pauline Scott. From Sister Scott's home, they moved to another storefront at 2925 Union Street, and shared space with the Church of Christ Holiness under Pastor Sims.

In 1948 they moved again to 721 Filbert Street where they shared space with the Mexican Baptist Church under Pastor Castineda. Dad's members held their services Sundays from 2:00 to 5:00 p.m. and on Thursday nights. Occasionally, they used other nights, as they were available. Dad's day job was at General Electric on East 14th.

Eventually, they found a large lot located on the northwest corner of 10th and Myrtle Streets. The lot was 95x95 for the price of $4,600. The congregation pooled their money for a down payment, bought the lot, and paid it off in a very short time. With a loan from the Church of God headquarters in Anderson, Indiana, construction of a permanent church home began in 1950. Church members built our church with their own hands: the men constructing and hammering, the women making tuna fish sandwiches with white bread along with strawberry Kool-Aid.

Dad, Aaron, Fritz, our uncles Jack and Leon, and our cousins,

Bill, Leon Jr., and Paul Silas carried stacks of lumber and buckets of nails. They worked tirelessly to create the white stucco building with a baptismal pool behind thick glass so the congregation could see the person being dunked underwater and lifted back up. On the back wall, there was this huge painting of Jesus being baptized by John the Baptist, with a raised arm that looked like it was coming out of John's neck instead of his shoulder.

By the mid-1950s, we all sang in the junior choir at our church named The West Oakland Church of God. All of us—Aaron, Fritz, me, Ruth, our cousins, Leon, Bill, and Paul Silas—formally auditioned and were placed in a row with other sopranos, altos, tenors, or basses. Our family was practically a choir just by ourselves. Brother James Hirt, the church pianist, was there to accompany most songs, or if he could not attend, we sang a cappella. We developed poise, self-confidence, and the ability to sing with feeling and power: to appreciate group singing, lyrics and harmony, and to provoke audience response. It was a true training ground for performing.

During this time, there were fifteen of us living in our single-family, two-story duplex. There were nine of us upstairs: Mom and Dad in one bedroom; me, Ruth, Bonnie ,and June in a room with two sets of bunkbeds; Papa (Daddy's dad), in a room with a window that overlooked the backyard; and Aaron and Fritz in bunk beds up against the west wall of the dining room.

The downstairs was not a part of the original house: the bathroom was outside underneath the stairs. Six people lived on the first floor: Uncle Leon and Aunt Clara Mae, Leon Jr., Bill, and Paul Silas, and Grandma Stevens (Grandma Roxie's 100-year-old mother, a full-blood Cherokee). We were all related and got along amazingly well except when Uncle Jack came by with some of his drunken foolishness: fighting with his brother, Leon, or pulling a knife on Daddy. You can't choose your relatives.

Some years later, Jack got saved and joined the choir at Marin City Church of God. "Music," Mother often quoted from the *Bible,* "will soothe the savage beast." In Uncle Jack's case, that's what we hoped!

Of course, there was no smoking or drinking alcohol upstairs or downstairs, and there were also no movies, radio, nail polish, dresses above the knee, going to parties, or dancing. When us kids did start sneaking out, it would not be long before Dad would track us down, even in dark corners of a house party or park-sponsored dance, armed with his trusty flashlight.

On Friday or Saturday evenings, some of us would go "fishing" with Mother and a couple of other "saints." That meant standing on the corner of 7th and Adeline Streets singing hymns like *Rescue the Perishing* and *I Cannot Be Idle*, or *Bringing in the Sheaves* while passing out "tracts," which were pamphlets with scriptures and daily affirmations such as: Philippians 4:8 (NIV), "Whatever is true, whatever is noble, whatever is right, whatever is pure, whatever is lovely, whatever is admirable—if anything is excellent or praiseworthy—think about such things."

In the late 1950s, there were still a lot of jobs in Oakland, especially West Oakland: companies like Carnation, Nabisco, Heinz, Coca-Cola, U.S. Steel, and Del Monte Cannery. Members of the church owned businesses as well: real estate, auto mechanic, dry cleaning, childcare, nursing home, painting, construction, and grocery stores. There were a couple of police officers (the Scott brother twins), lawyers, and even a doctor or two. They filled the church parking lot with beautiful Buicks, Pontiacs, Oldsmobiles, Fords, and even a Cadillac.

Sunday dinners were usually spectacular. Mother was an excellent cook because she truly loved it and because she had studied to be a dietitian in New York. She knew how to prepare a good, healthy meal for a lot of people on a small budget. Her specialties were greens, candied yams, red beans and rice, enchiladas, tamale pie, Spanish rice, battered shrimp, meat loaf and mashed potatoes, and baked macaroni and cheese. One of her most popular dishes was "The Gospel Bird" (fried chicken) and perhaps for dessert banana pudding, coconut cake, pineapple upside-down cake, German chocolate cake, or sweet potato pie. And then there was always the possibility of hand-stirred, homemade ice cream with unequaled, incomparable taste. Have mercy!

Like so many women we saw around us, she was hard-working and dedicated to her family. When the church wasn't doing so well financially, which happened quite often, Mother, Sister Lee, and Sister Reed would get on one of the work trucks parked near Swans Department Store, and go to Fresno or Modesto to pick strawberries and green beans with the Mexican workers in order to feed us. She also did "day work" for a couple of white families in Piedmont. She took the bus there, believing in the proverb "An idle mind is the devil's workshop." She was not afraid of work, and that steadfast ethic made us unafraid of work.

Our father was a man of tremendous dignity. We heard only the best of language, never a curse word or even a raised voice to us, or our mother. "Hotzigady" he would say, reacting to some mishap or mistake, or "that's bass-ackward" when something was not done as it should have been. He treated everyone with respect. He visited and prayed for and anointed the sick. He dressed impeccably. Daddy was also a man of tremendous integrity and discipline. After his epiphany and transformation, his "salvation" in 1935 and baptism in 1936, he never smoked nor drank alcohol, and was a faithful husband to our mother, a loving father, and a positive role model for his congregation.

He was a fantastic preacher: eloquent, erudite, animated, and passionate. Dad worked hard, and he read voraciously. Without a typewriter or typist at his disposal, he wrote out every sermon, long-hand. He built a library for himself in the basement of our house at 18th and Adeline Streets, across the street from DeFremery Park. Even when we moved to Oakland Avenue, he built a library there as well. Mother said, "I don't think he's seen a book that he doesn't want to buy."

Chapter 3
THE MAKE∫HIFT MICROPHONE

"**B**ONNIE" WAS BORN, PATRICIA EVA, JULY 11, 1950, AT HIGHLAND Hospital in Oakland, California. She was the penultimate one, fifth in the line of six. "Bonnie" got her nickname from Brother James and Sister Lilian Hirt, who babysat her one summer when Mom and Dad went to Arkansas for a visit with Grandma Roxie and Granddaddy Fritz. Brother Hirt was the church pianist and a mailman. Sister Hirt, for Fritz, was love at first sight. Describing Patricia one day, she said, "She's cute as a bunny." *Bunny* somehow got transformed into *Bonnie* by Bonnie: "I did it myself" she said. "I like the idea of naming myself, like making myself. I'm the only one in the family with a nickname."

November 30, 1953, June Antoinette was born at Highland Hospital. She was the last of six siblings, the baby sister. June and Fritz were decade twins, born exactly ten years, to the day, apart. They had a special affinity and bond.

Just like she did with all of us girls, Mother would sing June to sleep with her sweet voice. June had a good musical ear and sang in the junior choir. Dad wanted to protect his talented daughters from the "devil's music," and the temptation-ridden life of the blues and jazz world. There was one radio and Dad *owned* that; it was his. It was exclusively for news and gospel music, on Sunday, that's it. Eventually, we got a stereo, a Motorola combination TV and record player. Mom had a Mahalia Jackson record she pulled out during holidays; and that was it for records in the house.

I really felt like we were being shut out, not allowed to listen to anything but gospel. I would go to my friends' houses and listen to as much as I could. I would even cut out of a church youth meeting or something so I could go to someone's house and listen to as much rock n' roll and R&B music as I could. I didn't understand why we couldn't listen to it. I just thought it was ridiculous.

I'm sure it was my parents' way of protecting us. At home there were no loud, angry arguments, no cussing and fighting, no chaos. Mother never was social, in a secular or "worldly" sort of way. She never danced; nor did tobacco or alcohol ever touch her lips—the church even used grape juice for communion—she never did any of that stuff. She had been "saved" and a Christian since age twelve.

Mother really had a big heart. She worked hard doing domestic work for white families in Piedmont, California; she went to the fields in Modesto or Fresno with Sister Lee to pick vegetables or fruit. We knew she struggled, and she really didn't ask for much. As we grew up, we always shopped at second-hand and thrift stores. One particular holiday season there was a suggestion that the congregation purchase a new outfit for her. They literally took a vote on that, and it was a big deal.

"Daddy and Mom were great," Bonnie said. "I was under Mom's apron strings. I was in the kitchen with her all the time, because I liked cooking: that's why I can cook now. Daddy taught me about life—how to be a good person; he was a beautiful father. He was a gentle and kind soul. He and mom were really the greatest parents anybody could have. Do you know what it must have been like to raise six kids, all supercharged in their own right? Can you imagine how hard that was?"

In those early years, despite the tight finances, Dad and Mom bought an upright piano and expected one of us to take lessons and learn how to play it. Fritz started with a teacher on 27th and Market for a dollar per lesson, learned finger position, the over and under scale thing, but he was distracted by a nearby Doggie Diner and the dollar started going for chili dogs and soft-serve ice cream cones.

I was singing in various church choirs along with my sisters from the time we could walk. The first church choir was called Little Soldiers. We wore these poncho-looking outfits with red edging and big red bows on the front as we marched around the church singing, "We are little soldiers, marching off to war." Of course, all of us were expected, as pastors' kids, to participate in most, if not all, church activities. Singing was something we were happy to do! We all attended

Sunday school, Vacation Bible School, Junior Choir rehearsal, and summer camp meetings.

Oakland, at that time, was really a city of opportunity. It was just after World War II: there were servicemen and women all over; there were Naval bases in Oakland and Alameda. At this time, in the fifties, we were also a close-knit community in many ways: we not only walked to church, we walked to school, we walked to the store, and to visit our friends. On the way, we met friends and neighbors and church folk. We knew a house where gays lived, and another where lesbians lived. We looked for antennae to see who had televisions and who didn't.

The people in the church and the DeFremery personnel were excellent role models for us: self-employed, or gainfully employed, independent, educated, and trained men and women. We liked the way they dressed, with a certain élan, at least on Sunday, and we wanted to dress like that. For Daddy, every day was Sunday. He didn't own a pair of jeans or tennis shoes. If not in a tie, every day he was in a dress shirt, slacks, and shined shoes.

We had respect for members, especially the elders, of the church. We would never call someone by a first name. It was Sister Tires, not Willie Mae; it was Sister Lee, not Imogene; it was Brother Hirt, not James. This was as important to them as it was to us. The foot-washing ceremonies and testimony services at the church added to this sense of a tight little community. "Sins" were supposed to be openly confessed before the entire congregation.

When we weren't in church, or school, we were at DeFremery Park. That was our babysitter, our home away from home. There was just so much to do: swings and slides and merry-go-rounds, paddleball and tennis courts and a swimming pool where, believe it or not, we witnessed Olympic-level diving and synchronized swimming performances, under the lights on a cool summer California evening.

There were also basketball courts, where future NBA stars like Bill Russell, Paul Silas, and Joe Ellis honed their skills. There was a baseball field where, under the evening lights, we watched fast-pitch softball, and witnessed three of the top seven hitters in the National League, in 1961, with at least 350 plate appearances, come from McClymonds High; Frank Robinson, Vada Pinson, Curt Flood, and our brother Aaron developed into record-breaking professionals in the MLB.

The park used to be a USO (United Service Organization) center for servicemen and women. There were rooms for pool and ping-pong; bands played, and dances were held. It was a recreation and social hall. It was a big, beautiful, three-story Victorian mansion right in the center of the park with eucalyptus magnolia and oak trees scattered around it.

I was in Cooking, Arts and Crafts, and Charm classes. We were taught good team spirit, how to win or lose graciously; proper etiquette while dining; good posture while walking with books on our heads; or sitting with legs crossed just so at the ankles; even how to enter and exit a car without giving away the store—all of which now comes automatically. Park Director Dorothy Pitts and dance teacher extraordinaire, Ruth Beckford, both had a positive impact on me. I could never forget the Maypole dances, the Hokey-Pokey, swimming lessons, water shows, and the day John F. Kennedy came to DeFremery.

That magical park played a significant role in our lives and in our careers as entertainers, athletes, and educators. Those activities kept us occupied and out of trouble. It had so many different levels...the reading room was near the front door. You could do so many different things. You could go upstairs to play ping pong, or cards, or dominoes, or shoot pool. There was another ping pong table downstairs and sofas and big soft chairs in the lounge; there was a kitchen and a serving area with a bar. We would just sit in the Club room and relax and talk and make grand plans for the future.

Without realizing it, we were learning lessons that we would eventually apply to our career as The Pointer Sisters. We were always told that we could succeed, and we could be successful if we worked hard. That message was ingrained in us at a young age, and we took it seriously.

Our neighborhood was mostly black, mostly poor working-class, although there were white people on one side of us, on 18th Street. A man named Frank lived next door, and he and his family were one of the only whites on the block. I never knew their last name, but they had a huge windmill in the backyard. Frank also made wine. Around the same time every year, we could smell it all over the neighborhood.

THE MAKE∫HIFT MICROPHONE

We also had grape vines and a fig tree in our own backyard. And, Papa, our grandfather, grew corn and raised rabbits.

Sometimes, when there were evening dances or other social events, fights would break out. Dad would often go over and try to separate the angry men. He was usually successful. He was never injured or anything, but we still worried for him. He took it upon himself to monitor the neighborhood for trouble. He kept a pair of binoculars near the big front window. He would watch people in the park, and if anyone appeared to be getting heated, he would grab his *Bible* and head out the door to smooth things out.

Mother told him, "Somebody's going to hit you on the head if you don't stay out of people's business."

We also had a public phone number, listed in the phone book, because Dad said, "We're going to keep an open line in case someone is in trouble and needs prayer or help in some way." It didn't matter who or when, Dad would help people at all times of the day and night.

Church was our life. We did what we were told, participated in church activities, and contributed to the ministry as much as we could. But as we got older, we really wanted to get out of all those church rules and regulations: no sports on Sundays, no lipstick, no movies, no dances, no parties, and no music except church music—it was like being in jail. Especially the part about no secular music!

We had a desire to be adventurous and do the things we saw our other friends doing like going to movies or school dances. It seemed like the kids who were not in our church were having much more fun than we were having. We tried to abide by the ideas, rules, and regulations our parents preached about and truly lived. We wanted to become "real Christians" and even tried to recruit others to our church.

On the other side of us were the Raposas, an Italian family. Patsy Raposa was my best friend until we moved away to 408 Oakland Avenue when I was 12 years old. We went to elementary school together. But her mother and father were so strict with her that they wouldn't let her out of the yard after school. They had a driveway on one side of their house and a chain link fence and a gate. Every day, we played at the gate, with her on one side and me on the other. We'd sit there and play for hours with that gate separating us. It was all we knew. Patsy was not allowed out, and I was not allowed in. That rule was only broken on Patsy's birthday. Then I could actually go inside! Our family went to church and the park, but Patsy couldn't even go across the street. I think her father was afraid of West Oakland and wanted to protect her. It was strange, but we made it work. I wish I knew what ever happened to my little friend.

We felt safe in the park and around the neighborhood. Aaron and Fritz were star athletes known throughout the community. In fact, we were called "The Pointer brothers' sisters!" When we were younger, they got bicycles and we didn't. I always had to borrow one of my brothers' bikes. My mother would tell us she thought it was too dangerous for girls to have one, but we thought it was because she couldn't afford to buy one for each of us. When they were older, they got to stay out later and even use Dad's car sometimes. At the park, they played basketball games into the late evening, under the lights with some of the guys in the neighborhood.

Aaron was really popular, even voted high school student body president for the 1958-59 school year, an all-city baseball and basketball player, and an A student. The McClymonds High basketball team went five years without losing a game. From the years 1958 to 1962, McClymonds High School, arguably, was the greatest high school basketball team of all time. No high school team has ever accomplished what "Mack" did. Not Crispus Attucks, with the great Oscar Robinson, nor Overbrook High School, with Wilton (Wilt) Chamberlain, nor Power Memorial with Lewis Alcindor (now Kareem Abdul Jabbar).

From 1958 to 1962, Mack's teams attained a record of 110 wins and merely one loss. Over a three-year period that began in 1958 and stretched to 1961, this team was undefeated with a record of 66 wins and no defeats. As a result, they were voted the *mythical* National Champions, the best high school team in America. That was for three consecutive years. No other school can boast such an achievement. Over five consecutive years, they were California's best team, no one even came close. Paul Silas was the State Player of the Year, and his cousin, our brother Fritz, led the '59 and '60 teams.

I used to sit in the window watching the kids heading for McClymonds. I wanted to go to Mack so badly. Every morning a lot of kids would stop by our house and Mother would fix breakfast for them. But we moved when I was twelve, and I ended up going to Oakland Tech. Dad no longer worked at General Electric on East 14th and was full time with the church. Mother and Aunt Clara Mae worked as cooks in the Laney College cafeteria. Later, Mother worked at Del Monte Cannery and then got a job as a janitor with the City of Oakland at the Oakland Public Library. I remember going with her to clean the main library, near Lake Merritt. It was at night, and felt kind of spooky, even with other janitors there.

We first started singing at home, and then of course at church. We began in the Junior Choir then moved to the Senior Choir. I would sing all the time around the house and so did Mother. She loved to sing. When she would send me to the store for something, I'd make up a little song about it so I wouldn't have to write it down; and I'd sing: "Got to get milk, bread, a pound of butter," all the way to the store.

I would also sing along to records when I visited my friends' houses. My favorite song was "The Lady is a Tramp." I would sing duets with one of my sisters, for our aunts and uncles, too; one of our favorite hymns was "The Blood" written by Andrae Crouch. Like a lot of little girls, I dreamed of being on stage. Of course, I didn't know if it would happen, but I knew I wanted to be a singer.

Even though we weren't supposed to, as soon as Mom and Dad left us at home alone, for a prayer or usher board meeting or choir practice, we turned on the radio and heard The Platters singing "Only You" and "The Great Pretender"; Elvis singing "Heartbreak Hotel"; Sam Cooke with "You Send Me"; Nina Simone pouring her heart out with "I Loves You Porgy"; and Etta James with her powerful song, "All I Could Do Was Cry." The goal was to squeeze in as much music as we could before Mom and Dad got home.

I would tuck my dress up into my panties and use the piano bench as a stage, the pie pans as tambourines, and a gold, athletic trophy— plucked from the polished wooden piano top crowded with family photographs—as a microphone. We would take turns putting on a show. It was magical.

There was no television for much of our childhood, so we entertained each other. One of us kept lookout at the big front living room window, where we could see as far as 16th Street, to watch out for Dad's two-tone, white on top and grey on the bottom, 1955 Buick. Once it was spotted, we broke into teams of two or three to get the dishes washed and put away before they reached the front driveway.

Saturdays were also preparation for Sundays: haircuts for the boys, with manual clippers; for the girls, hot-comb-straightening and curling of hair; and for all, ironing, bathing, polishing shoes, and reading Sunday school lessons. On Christmas, Easter, Valentine's, and Thanksgiving Sundays, we had poems, recitations to memorize and perform. The older we got, the longer the poems.

There were everyday clothes and shoes and Sunday clothes and shoes. Aaron, Fritz, Bill ("Pie"), Leon Jr., and Paul wore suits and ties, sometimes bowties, to church. Sunday mornings we walked to church, in time for 9:00 Sunday school, about eight blocks away. On rainy days, we all piled into Daddy's big Buick: big kids on the bottom, smaller kids on laps. Sometimes, during evening services, Bonnie and I would sneak away to hear Billy Preston and Andrae Crouch singing—that kind of singing, that kind of enthusiastic, rhythmic and harmonic music and singing—accompanied by drums, lead and bass guitar, and piano. We loved Ephesians' Church of God in Christ "Midnight Musicals." They were "musicals" with shouters, high-steppers, tongue speakers, and more!

Sometimes during the summer, all of us would travel by car to Prescott, Arkansas to visit with Granddaddy Fritz and Grandma Roxie, and stay in their big house on the corner of Green Lawn Street. Daddy packed these huge lunches and Mother and Sister Reed boxed and stored fried chicken. There wouldn't be much stopping; Jim Crow was still the order of the day, and "fast food" was whatever you could order from the back door of a restaurant or carry in a box.

One year, Sister Reed (who was a large woman) came with me to Arkansas. Sometimes, one of us would ride on the ledge of the rear window just to have more space. Dad had what was called a *Green Book* that black people carried when they traveled by car that gave them directions to friendly and "decent" accommodations, auto repair shops, and even doctors. We stopped at a motel once and there were big moths flying around the door. Everyone got in but me, and they wouldn't open the door to let me in! Daddy had some kind of insect phobia, for real, and would not open that door.

The first trip I remember taking was to Prescott, Arkansas. I begged to go there to stay for a while and attend the fifth grade there so it must have been around 1958. It was like being in some wild, un-civilized place. I mean, people were living in little shacks, all over the place, with no heating, no running water, and no washing machines, no indoor toilets. And I thought we were poor back in California! But compared to this? I understood why Mother would take some of our Christmas gifts and send them down there to Grandma Roxie to pass out to some of these families.

There were rats in the rafters of Ms. Curtistine's house; I could hear them running around, turds would just drop down in my lap. The water faucet was outside. Now, the second time I went, they had moved the water faucet inside, a big improvement. Still, where the water was running, it had eaten a hole in the floor. I could see right through to the ground.

Some children only had shoes for school in the winter, and in the summer, they went barefoot. They even played on gravel barefoot. I wanted to fit in and took off my shoes and tried, but I couldn't do it. You have to be used to that sort of thing. I used to help them do their laundry. They made their own soap—these big, ol' chunks of lye soap—and they had a scrub board and a big, ol' round tub out in the backyard. You'd think it was the turn of the century, but this was actually the 1950s.

One day, my grandmother let me go pick cotton. I thought it was fun until I found out how much cotton you had to pick to get one dollar. The bag would be 25 feet long, and you had to fill it up. Twice! It was a learning experience for me, but I saw people out there with their families trying to make money for their livelihoods. It was a learning experience.

The schools were segregated, and the black school had leaking ceilings. When it rained, we had to run around the classroom and put buckets all over the place. We also had to wash the windows in the school. They didn't even have a science lab at the black school like the white school had.

In downtown Prescott, there were signs on the water faucets, "Colored" on one side and "White" on the other side. My friends and I would go downtown and drink on the white side and then run away just to make the townspeople mad. At the movie theaters, we couldn't go in the front door. We had to go to the back and up these stairs to the balcony. It was the same thing in restaurants: you couldn't go to the front door. You had to go pick up your food on the side. I couldn't believe it.

FAIRYTALE

Oh, my goodness, it was such a different place than Oakland, California. I went back to Prescott for the seventh grade and the tenth grade, so I experienced elementary, junior high, and high school there. I loved it there. I loved the people—many of them. I loved the smell of the place and the whole country vibe. But it took some getting used to.

Bonnie came with me to Arkansas when I went for the seventh grade, but she didn't stay the whole year. She did stay through Halloween. Grandma Roxie had to tell us that this was the South and not California. We had to be back home before dark. There was a black side of town and a white side of town; Granddaddy Fritz and Grandma Roxie's house was on Green Lawn Street, which separated the two sides.

I remember trick-or-treating, not far from Grandma's house, when a pick-up truck full of white boys pulled up and jumped out swinging chains and crowbars, saying: "We gonna kill some niggers today." Bonnie and I took off running in different directions. We were so frightened that we didn't even think. We just ran! We were actually running away from the house. Next thing I knew, I was in the woods, scared as I could be. I was trying to get over a fence when they caught me. Then all they did was hand me a bag of candy. I guess they just wanted to scare us. Then they even gave me the wrong directions. I was alone, but I somehow ended up at Aunt Hattie and Uncle James' house in Channey on the other side of town.

Despite those events, I liked going to Arkansas. I guess it was because I felt like an only child when I was there. That made me feel special. Granddaddy Fritz even taught me how to drive and I got my first driver's license at age twelve!

At home, in Oakland, I thought of myself as an oddball. I was fat; I wore glasses, and I was light-skinned. Nobody else in the family looked like me. I even wrote a letter to myself saying how I was going to stay with my grandma because nobody liked me. My brothers and sisters teased me and talked about me, really tortured me: they called me Sitting Bull, Four Eyes, The Fat One, all kinds of names.

Even though I knew they were just trying to annoy me, that insecurity about my weight and looks always stayed with me. So, I enjoyed getting away from them sometimes. At Grandma's I would have my own room, there was always enough to eat, and when I put things in the fridge and went back for them, they were still there. I was so busy when I was there that I always lost weight.

Chapter 4

ORANGE CRUSH

IN THE SUMMER OF 1961, BONNIE AND I, ALONG WITH A COUPLE OF Mother's friends, went to Arkansas in an eighteen-wheeler, you know, one of those moving trucks. These church friends had furniture they were taking with them, so it was like a little apartment in the back of this moving van. We went all the way from Oakland to Arkansas in that truck.

I was in the seventh grade and Bonnie was in fifth, but she stretched the truth a little. She remembers, "I told them I was in sixth, and was in a sixth-grade class, and doing the work; until my transcripts came from Oakland and they found out I was really in fifth grade. Well, I was sent back home, to Oakland, and placed where I belonged."

I spent the whole year there with Grandma Roxie and Grand-daddy Fritz. Then I returned to Oakland for the eighth grade and attended West Lake Jr. High School. I sang in the choir, and I loved it. I had the best teacher you could have. Ms. Gillette, our choral teacher, was so wonderful and taught me a lot of things that I used throughout my professional career, like using my diaphragm and bringing notes up from my stomach, my gut, and putting the final "T" of a word in a song on the next word, like "swee...tand kind." In later years, Ms. Gillette moved to Germany and believe it or not, when we were performing there, she actually came to the show!

I was also on the West Lake cheerleading squad and even sewed together the cheerleaders' uniforms of green and white with a big green block-letter "W" on a white sweater and green corduroy skirts. Our squad was a bit chubby though. In fact, the guys used to yell at us, "You need to go out on the field and play on the team!"

ORANGE CRUSH

In the early 60s, I attended Oakland Technical High School. I didn't get to sing as much as I had in other grades. Actually, I didn't do any singing in high school. I was in drama and acted in plays. I had the role of Lady Macbeth and really liked that play. Thomas Whayne, my drama teacher at Tech, was also fantastic. We did *A Raisin in the Sun*. What a wonderful play, and still a relevant story. He took us on field trips, to see plays like one by The Committee, an avant-garde San Francisco improv group that talked about masturbation, sexuality, politics, and stuff like that. I must admit I had a crush on Mr. Whayne, a gorgeous man. He still sends me a Christmas card every year.

Ted Lange, who became an actor known mostly for playing the role of "Isaac" on *The Love Boat,* went to my school, and we were in plays together like *Macbeth* and Thornton Wilder's *The Skin of Our Teeth.* We fancied ourselves "serious" thespians among other things. I was very active at Oakland Tech and joined every committee and group I could join: Chairman of the Senior Ball Committee, member of Student Senate; Delphians Honor Society for Scholastic B-plus all three years; and Thespian Honor Society for Theater. Although I was busy, I wasn't that popular. I was just involved and really into school activities. In later years, I had the opportunity to appear with Ted on *The Love Boat* with a script he had written. That was truly coming full circle!

I remember when 13-year-old genius Stevie Wonder came out with the song *Fingertips Part II* (1963) I just said, if *this* is a sin, then I'm a sinner. I couldn't be a hypocrite. I loved that song. Why should I pretend that I didn't like that "worldly" music? How could I lie to myself about how it made me feel? What *god* would want me to lie to myself about this? I loved Stevie Wonder and still do. I love his music. When I got a copy of his record in high school, I hugged it to my chest and dreamed of him. If that meant I was not "saved," it was a risk I was willing to take. I didn't get up and make a statement or anything like that; it was what I felt inside. It was what I truly believed, and it was a turning point in my life.

Along with not listening to secular music, there were other rules that I found unfair. Girls couldn't wear pants to school; we could only wear dresses and skirts, and I thought that was ridiculous, especially on rainy days and when it was cold. Who made up this silly rule? I wanted to wear pants to school.

FAIRYTALE

In the mid 1960s, Bonnie or Ruth and I would attend the "Midnight Musicals" at Ephesians Church of God in Christ. It was eye-opening to see a completely different interpretation of gospel music, by folks like Billy Preston and Andrae Crouch. They were performing "rock-out" gospel songs and word was spreading in the community. They sort of shook things up at our church by dividing the congregation. The elders did not embrace the lively gospel sound. They wanted to keep the emotion out of the music. The younger members found it exciting and were leading the charge.

At Ephesians, recall they had drums, guitars, tambourines, pianos, and organs backing the singers. The more energetic, rhythmic gospel music had people, literally, dancing in the aisles. I loved this whole period of harmonic group singing, and the elegant style of dressing that went with it: The Andrews Sisters' "Bei Mir Bist Du Schon" (To Me You Are Beautiful) and "Boogie Woogie Bugle Boy"; The McGuire Sisters' "Sincerely"— they also happened to be Church of God, like us. We genuinely loved silk and chiffon dresses, stylish jackets and pants, well-made comfortable shoes, and fancy hats, what some would call *antique* clothing: that old quality stuff.

Throughout high school, I was very insecure as a girl, and I'm sure that's why I didn't have boyfriends. I really didn't think anybody liked me, not even my sisters. I felt I was ugly, the fat girl who wore glasses. Ironically, I was head of the senior prom committee, and I couldn't get a date. Nobody asked me, and everybody I asked turned me down. This was in June of '65. In May of that year, I had met a boy named David at a party. He seemed like a nice guy, so I called him. He was much older, but I went out with him anyway and ended up getting drunk on screwdrivers—vodka and orange juice. I was a virgin. I was seventeen. And the unthinkable happened.

When I got home that night, I was still bleeding a lot. Mother said, "I told you to keep your dress down." The bleeding and pain were just horrible. I lay in bed in puddles of blood for what felt like several days. Mother and Sister Lee looked after me as best they could. After they saw I wasn't getting any better, Mother took me to the hospital. I had a split uterus and had to go to my graduation in a wheelchair. I was Miss Goody, Goody Two-Shoes, not having had sex throughout high school, when a lot of the other girls were. Then that happened.

To make matters worse, after passing my ACT and SAT exams and being accepted to Howard University, I found out I was pregnant. I was 17. I really, deeply believed that this was the end of all my dreams of college, of singing; I would just end up a mother and housewife. Of course, my parents were disappointed. Several members of the church were especially critical and mean to them. "What kind of pastor can't even control his own daughters?" "How can they lead the church and can't lead their family?" Not long after that, the church officials asked our father to step down as pastor.

Those horrible events did not help my self-esteem. I thought my life was over. College was out of the question. I had no idea what I would do. Long ago I had promised myself I wouldn't be a housekeeper or an office worker. I wanted something different. I had dreams, and I felt like I had just messed up everything. For a long time, after that horrible night with the screwdrivers, just the smell of oranges made my stomach turn.

So, I did what I thought I had to do. I got married. He took classes at Merritt College and drove a truck delivering medical supplies and equipment. I was at a club one evening when I was eight months pregnant. I shouldn't have been out, but there I was. My husband had told me he was out of town delivering medical equipment. All of a sudden, he walked in with this floozy and all hell broke loose. It was during those years when women blamed other women and never the man. I ended up going home with him in that stupid truck. I never really knew him, and he never knew me.

I wasn't afraid of hard work, and there were employment and training opportunities in Oakland and San Francisco. Oakland had been chosen as a Model City and there were programs like the OIC (Opportunities Industrialization Center) and EOC (Economic Opportunity Council). They would actually provide paid training for all kinds of jobs. I improved my secretarial, typing, shorthand, offset press, and PBX switchboard skills with classes and practice there. I learned to appreciate punctuality, responsibility, and organization. They sent me to A.B. Dicks' training school for office equipment that they must have known would be obsolete in a few years and replaced by computers. Despite my vow to not be an office worker, I loved operating the archaic PBS switchboard, and it felt like I was on an episode of *I Love Lucy*. I eventually found a job working at a law office, and even typed up my own divorce decree.

My brothers were older and focused on their own promising futures. Aaron was high school class president, and both were star athletes. They dated all the pretty girls and had clothing accounts funded by working summer jobs. Fritz got into trouble his last year of junior high and spent a year in reform school. It changed his life. When he got out, he had a new set of friends and became a good student and athlete. Both received athletic scholarships to attend universities: Aaron went to the University of San Francisco and Fritz to Creighton University in Omaha, Nebraska. In 1962, Aaron was drafted out of college to play professional baseball for the Houston Colt 45s. Good thing too, because his son Derek was born October 9, 1961.

He played on the first team to have all rookies in the starting lineup. He was, as of 2020, the last professional baseball player to bat .400 for a season: a record unbroken in 50 years. He came up to the major league for a short time; his team was playing the Giants in San Francisco. Unfortunately, I had *no* chance to see him play.

I was working at the law offices of Metoyer and Sweeny, in Berkeley, and they wouldn't let me have the day off. He had played in Venezuela and a few years in Japan. Deron, his second son, was born in Japan on September 9, 1971. When we performed in Japan, in the early 70s, Aaron was well known. Before leaving there, Aaron was stopped at the airport to go through a formal ceremony apologizing for taking his son out of the country.

For many years, Aaron has been Commissioner of Parks and Recreation, an elected position, in Tacoma, Washington. He was also an NFL referee for quite a few years before he retired. It was so special when Ruthie, June, and I sang the National Anthem for an L.A. Raiders game and Aaron was officiating.

Our cousin, Paul Silas, one of the sons of Uncle Leon (our mother's brother), grew up in the same house with us. He graduated from Creighton University and became a professional basketball player and NBA coach. Paul said DeFremery Park was where he got introduced to organized sports. "They didn't have anything like that in Arkansas, certainly not Prescott. Playing basketball late into the evening, under the park lights was an unforgettable experience. It was the most fun time I ever had in my life."

Fritz, Paul, and Paul's older brother, William ("Pie") attended Creighton at the same time. The year they played together (1963-64) Creighton's basketball team had the best year in the school's history. Family lore has it that Creighton wanted Paul so badly they gave his brother Pie, who didn't even play basketball, a scholarship along with cousin Fritz. Unfortunately, Pie actually died while a student at Creighton.

Pie reminded me of R.P. McMurphy, Jack Nicholson's character in *One Flew Over the Cuckoo's Nest* (1975), except, Pie didn't survive the shock therapy. We heard he got upset in the student dining room one evening and began smashing and breaking things. So, Pie was taken to the hospital. The day Paul and Fritz went to see him, he told them, "If they keep me here, I'm going to die." We found out the "doctors" were actually giving him those electric shock treatments and, as a result, the following day he was dead. Pie was twenty-four when that happened. It was so quick and mysterious, so *accidental.*

After he graduated from Creighton with a degree in Management in 1964, Paul played for the St. Louis Hawks. Later, he played with the Boston Celtics and the Seattle Super Sonics, and won three NBA championships: two with the Boston Celtics in 1974 and 1976, and one with the Seattle Super Sonics in 1979.

When he was coaching the San Diego Clippers, the owner was Donald Sterling, who had achieved infamy for his racist words and behavior. Paul told of a little incident that confirmed Sterling's bigotry. Paul reported: "I had been given the head coach's office, of course. But, the second day I returned and found I had been moved to another office so one of Sterling's bimbos could have my office...because she liked it."

Paul coached for the San Diego Clippers and was head coach for the Phoenix Suns and Charlotte Hornets. He coached the Cleveland Cavaliers during LeBron James' first year as a pro. Paul is only one of five men in NCAA history to average 20 points and 20 rebounds in his college career; in 2017 he was inducted into the College Basketball Hall of Fame.

Then there's my brother Fritz. When he graduated from Creighton University in 1966, he had several offers to play professional basketball including the St. Louis Hawks, Detroit Pistons, and even The Harlem Globetrotters. Instead, he became a political activist and

FAIRYTALE

academic. He and Pastor Joseph Barndt wrote and got a $10,000 grant from The American Lutheran Church for a Cultural Center he started in North Oakland. Pastor Barndt noticed there were two Lutheran churches not too far from each other, so he turned one of them over to Fritz, who turned it into a Cultural Center, at 42nd and what is now Martin Luther King Way.

Fritz also attended UCLA and UW Madison for graduate degrees. He was a college professor for thirty years and published two books. He taught at Contra Costa College: English and African Studies. He really was a great teacher because he loved doing it. I've learned so much from him. He came back to Oakland with all this information about African History, Literature, and Religion, so he started a free Study Group.

If you wanted to come and didn't have a way, he'd pick you up. In those free classes, he taught me more about our history than I ever learned in public school. Going to school in Oakland, the only thing we ever learned about black people was that we were slaves and picked cotton, and that one guy, George Washington Carver, invented peanut butter. That was it! No culture, no nations or empires, no poets or poetry, no great men or women of history. That was all! I was like, "Come on. This is cold-blooded. Schools won't even teach us our true history."

He thought it was important for us to understand our lineage and accept our identity as Africans in America. He was an African History major at UCLA and an African Literature major at the University of Wisconsin. I loved learning from him about our past. Before he got the Center, he met in the homes of students and shared books and talk about African History and Politics. He started some of the first Black Student Unions and Black Studies Programs, in Bay Area high schools and colleges.

He enlisted help to do all the interior and exterior painting of the Center. Dominant colors were, of course, red, black, and green. They named it the Pan-African Cultural Center. We went to carpet stores and got scraps and put together patchwork carpets in a couple of the study rooms that had individual desks and lamps. He called it simply The Black Students Study Group.

Fritz knew about artists like Meta Warrick Fuller, Robert Duncanson, Romare Bearden, Elizabeth Catelett, Jacob Lawrence, and scientists like Lewis Latimer, Garret Morgan, and Dr. Charles Drew; he had read and could discuss books by W.E.B. DuBois, James Baldwin, Langston Hughes, Richard Wright, Toni Morrison, Angela Davis, Chinua Achebe, Ngugi Wa'Thiongo and Alex LaGuma, Aime Cesaire, and Frantz Fanon. I was impressed and fascinated.

The Black Student Study Group was open to anybody who wanted to come and discuss books and study together. We believed that knowledge was power; not guns or other weapons. The entire outside of the building was painted black; with florescent murals, on the west, MLK Drive side wall, of Malcolm X, Frederick Douglass, and W.E.B. Dubois. It was so cool.

Some of the guest speakers included Amiri Baraka (LeRoi Jones), Stokley Carmichael, and Maulana Karenga. We were acquainted with Bobby Seale, Huey Newton, and Eldridge Cleaver. They attended classes at the Center. Fritz's mentor, Dr. David "Mudavanha" Patterson (our adopted brother), was a great influence on his political awareness and thinking, and mine, too.

The African American social, political, and organizational infra-structure of Oakland in 1966 was highly developed. Mudavanha took Fritz to the offices and homes of members of the Urban League, NAACP, CORE, Afro-American Association, SNCC, the Nation of Islam, the Paul Robeson Society, RAM, and the Northern California Black Panther Party, and introduced him to their leadership. Fritz was advised not to join any of them, "but you should know who they are."

Mudavanha, which means "lover of all people," got his master's degree form SF State University and his Ph.D. from the University of California in Political Science. He was the first black man to work for IBM San Francisco. He had been to Africa, to Ghana, every year for the past twenty years. A brilliant man, his dissertation for UC Berkeley is titled: *The Constitution: An Exslave Interpretation.* He followed W.E.B. Dubois and was buried in Ghana.

By 1966, I was eighteen, married, and had been out of the family house for a year or so. My daughter, Jada, was born April 9, 1966, but I still took time to be involved in "the movement." Bonnie, Fritz, Barbara Paige (his then wife), and 1 helped to organize the first Black Power and Arts Conference in the state, maybe the country. It was held in San Francisco with big names in attendance like Maulana Karenga, Stokley Carmichael, Rap Brown, and playwright Ed Bullins.

I was so involved in the movement that I became an activist. Bonnie and I were amongst the first, if not *the* first, young black women in Oakland to wear afros. Mother started getting phone calls from church members saying they were praying for her and for us, wondering if we were on drugs and had lost our minds. We questioned why Jesus would be portrayed with blond hair, blue eyes and pale skin when *The Bible* described his hair as "like lamb's wool," and his "feet like burnt brass." We used *The Original African Heritage Study Bible* where all the prophets, including Moses, and Jesus, and the angels were portrayed as black. So, we understood why in other Bibles, He would look European even though He was not from Europe. People want *their gods* to look like them.

We wondered about talking snakes, and how Noah got polar bears and penguins on an ark in the middle of the desert; and the real big question: how a man dead for two thousand years could come back to life, literally. Now, a lot of people don't care to do anything about global warming because they believed these stories about a literal versus metaphorical resurrection. Ira Gershwin was right: "It ain't necessarily so, it ain't necessarily so. The things that you're liable to read in the *Bible* (or *Koran* or *Torah*, for that matter) it ain't necessarily so."

I was involved in an African fashion show. I helped to organize and present it. There was even a picture of me, somewhere, in African clothing. I didn't have a car, so I put Jada in a stroller and took a bus to San Francisco to attend Black Students Study Group meetings. We learned about Egypt and other great African empires. We took karate classes so we could defend ourselves "when the revolution comes."

People from Oakland became *Freedom Riders* to Lowndes County, Alabama, to support Fannie Lou Hammer and the "Original Black Panther Party" there, and people trying to exercise their right to vote. We believed in Black Power articulated by Stokely Carmichael and believed that black people should control the destiny of the black community. We were working with that Black Panther Party, the Northern California Black Panther Party: Dr. Ken Freeman, Dr. Isaac Moore, and Dr. Mudavanha.

We had meetings in San Francisco, in the basement apartment of one particular member where loud music was played in case there were listening devices. We huddled in a circle and read letters from

Carlos Moore in Cuba or Vincent Lynch in Tanzania. The Pan African Cultural Center helped plan and organize rallies with local and national speakers at DeFremery and Mosswood Parks; at McClymonds, Castlemount and Tech High schools; Merritt and Mills College and California College of the Arts auditorium; at Veteran Memorial auditoriums; and, in churches in Oakland and San Francisco. Young people from all over the Bay Area came to our Center.

We were just a few blocks from Marcus Bookstore (named after Marcus Garvey), one of the oldest African American bookstores in the United States. Julian and Raye Richardson, and their daughter, Blanch, the founding family, were our dear friends. We had no qualms about going there and spending a couple hundred dollars on books for the Center and ourselves when we could afford it. Our motto, displayed on a brochure we designed with our program and schedule included, was: Black Power Without Brain Power is Only Skin Deep.

We would take groups of friends with us to the Civil Rights meetings. It was at one of those meetings, I think, in Berkeley, that I met Stokely Carmichael and H. Rap Brown from the Student Nonviolent Coordinating Committee. Muhammad Ali even came and spoke to our Study Group. Those were some courageous times for us because we were young and thought we were invincible. We were going to change the world.

Things did get intense at times. We attended meetings with Black Panther leaders like Huey Newton, Bobby Seale, Eldridge and Kathleen Cleaver. The day after Bobby Hutton was at the Center, he was murdered by Oakland police. For weeks, the stench from the tear gas remained in the house where he was killed.

The Northern California Black Panther Party, in addition to conferences and rallies throughout the Bay Area, was also engaged in voter registration activities in San Francisco and Oakland. We used dances at our center and house parties to raise money. One unforgettable night, members of the Black Panther Party for Self-Defense, from Oakland, crashed a fund-raising party we were having in San Francisco, with guns blazing like lunatics and shouting: "We are the Black Panther Party for Self- Defense. Do not call yourselves Panthers again!" It was scary.

I also remember the night that Huey Newton got shot and had, allegedly, shot and killed an Oakland police officer: He was at our

Center, at a party we were having. He left the party and the next thing we heard was that Huey was shot. We organized a caravan of about seven cars and made our way to Highland Hospital. The police had surrounded the entrance and were standing in front of their cars pointing their rifles and guns at us, with dogs on leashes. I was so scared. I knew right then there had to be another way. We don't even have a safe hospital to take people to if they got wounded.

We also had enough sense to know that black people were not the majority. So, we decided to make a difference using creativity. Music, painting, literature and film, dance, and sports would be our weapons. What comes from the barrel of a gun is death. So, we were labeled "Cultural Nationalists," among other things. The Black Panther Party for Self-Defense (BPPSD) was, to us, "Violent Integrationists." They had the same goals as Martin Luther King Jr., but used violent means.

The BPPSD had copied the Ten-Point Platform of the Nation of Islam (NOI), but unlike the NOI, the BPPSD was fighting to integrate— violent integrationists. We first accepted that we were an African people, and preferred the ideas of Malcolm X, Marcus Garvey, W.E.B. Dubois, Kwame Nkrumah, and even Maulana Karenga and Kwame Toure. We focused on the power and premeditated use of culture to expedite our ideas. It seemed simple enough to us. We saw integration as a tactic for a better life, for some, not *the ultimate* goal for everybody. Unique cultural and ethnic communities were beautiful as long as they were not like the Ku Klux Klan. We visited Chinatown and Japan town in San Francisco. We were aware of Rosewood, Florida and Tulsa, Oklahoma's Black Wall Street, and the GAP Band, named after streets (Greenwood, Archer and Pine) in the historic Greenwood neighborhood.

We also organized a caravan of cars with Mudavanha and Aubrey and Abdul Labrie; Fritz had a '69 gold Pontiac GTO convertible and drove from Oakland to LA to hear the founder of the US organization, Dr. Maulana Karenga, speak. It was an easy trip to make. We were, in our own way, being revolutionary and representing "The Talented Tenth."

We sincerely respected Karenga's knowledge. Especially, when he spoke about the meaning of Kwanzaa or the 10th to 15th century empires of West Africa—Ghana, Mali, and Songhay—empires that were the size of the US, in West Africa before slavery, with universities like Sankore and Timbuktu. It was like a new language, a new identity: Karenga talked about 15th century Monomotapa and 16th century Great Zimbabwe. Such knowledge was always worth the trip to Los Angeles.

High school students in Oakland, at that time, and perhaps today, weren't learning about these civilizations. To hear Amiri Baraka read poetry was always an event like none other. The honesty and sincerity of his delivery could not be denied. The truths he conveyed could not be denied.

The thing that changed my mind about the Panthers was a few years later, in 1972, when they attacked Fritz, in his classroom. Now, he had gone to UCLA and studied African History, and he was teaching black students about Black History and they attack him. Beat him up really bad, in his classroom, almost killed him, and he was teaching to uplift black people. Well, I was completely through with Bobby and Huey and their thugs and anything they were doing or saying. Completely through!

So, this was the "love of the people" they were crowing about? Plus, we knew then, and we know now, that when men with guns start wearing uniforms and marching with pictures of a leader, it was all over. We wanted none of that. We were not about to be any-body's uniformed soldiers.

No lesser light than Albert Einstein put it this way: "That a man can take pleasure in marching in fours to the strains of a band is enough to make me despise him. He has only been given his big brain by mistake: unprotected spinal marrow was all he needed."

David Rubinson admited: "I knew about Anita, Bonnie, and June's involvement with the Black Panthers. I also knew that it was very dangerous, because the government had infiltrated the Panthers, and a significant number of their members were agent provocateurs and were causing problems." He continued, "When Fred Hampton was murdered in Chicago, that really sent a cold shiver through any-one who was active at the time. The system was saying to us, 'We are going to kill you. You can be lying in bed with your baby boy and we are going to break down your door and come in with machine guns and kill you.'"

While we were out trying to change the world, June and Bonnie had become very close. Wherever Bonnie went, June would show up, whether it was a party or the movies. Three years apart, June was really Bonnie's little sister, her little puppy dog. I was glad that they were so close. Bonnie also even helped me get voted into the school student government.

In 1966, still in high school, Bonnie got a scholarship to Mills College in Oakland for Creative Writing. She wrote poems and also did painting. One summer she was asked to attend California College of the Arts because of a pen and ink drawing she submitted to a contest. She lived in a campus dorm at Mills College for a semester as a member of the Upward Bound program. Mills had a gorgeous campus, and it was a great experience for her. She loved all the greenery and openness. She loved nature, art, music, and being creative.

Dad tried to keep all of his daughters' focus on the music of the gospel. That proved an impossible task in the vortex of music that the Bay Area had become in the late sixties. We were surrounded by a wildly rushing current and rich melting pot of musical styles, but Daddy wanted our focus to be on gospel music. So, that worldly music would be after Sunday school and *Bible* study and choir practice, and youth prayer meetings, and ensemble rehearsals for junior choir. The thinking of church members at the time was to either sing God's music or the devil's music.

Though tiny and thin, June filled a room with her smile and genuine laughter. With her quick wit and loose sense of humor, to us and to her friends, she was a joy to be around. She loved McDonald's cheeseburgers and Orange Crush, Halloween and birthdays. She was a light everywhere she went but didn't need or demand all the attention. We were all tall girls, and June was no exception. At age fifteen, she was shooting up; but with slightly protruding front teeth, June didn't see herself as "pretty." Mom and Dad were certainly in no position to afford braces since the church had basically fired Dad in 1967, suggesting that he and Mom couldn't control their own daughters who insisted on singing the devil's music. Also, his eyes were getting bad so I think they felt that he could no longer excite them like they needed. He got a little plaque to hang on the wall to remind him of the church he had helped to build with his own hands. He finally agreed. "As time went by, various little things made me realize that I'd served my time, that I had given them all I had for 22 years."

However, he had no pension and our income took a serious hit. Mother went to work as a janitor for the City of Oakland, and Daddy found a job as a "security guard" at an apartment complex. They lost the beautiful six-bedroom home on a hill, on Oakland Avenue, and were forced to move into a two-bedroom house on 92nd Avenue, in a rough part of East Oakland. Not only was the house smaller, but Bonnie, June, and Faun, Ruth's three-year-old daughter, still lived with them.

Then tragedy struck our family and we never truly recovered from the repercussions. One evening, in the summer of 1968, while returning home from a neighborhood store on an errand for Mother, out of nowhere, June was attacked and brutally raped by several black males, as our niece Faun witnessed the whole horrible event. I don't want to go into the details because it still haunts us to this day, but it affected June and the whole family for the rest of our lives.

We didn't go to the police, because we had seen that it rarely, if ever, did any good. The neighborhood was a rough area where we knew that we had to fend for ourselves, and that's what we did. Fritz and Mudavanha took a rifle and a .357 Magnum, jumped into Fritz's orange Volvo, and went looking for the rapists. I guess for all of us it's a good thing they didn't find the thugs because that would not have turned out well. Unfortunately, the trauma of that event stayed with June and affected her severely.

I think June may have felt that she was at a disadvantage because she was the youngest. Our older brothers weren't always around by that point, so there was no one to protect her. By that time, Fritz was 25, married, living in Berkeley and working for Bechtel Corporation in San Francisco as an Administrative Assistant. Aaron was playing professional baseball somewhere in North Carolina.

June had heard stories of how Fritz had fought for Ruthie and beat up some boy for bothering with her, and how Aaron had stood up for Fritz and "whooped a couple of asses" on his behalf. However, June never had that. She was only 15 at the time of the attack and maybe she would have been safer if we were there, closer, known in that community, but circumstances had changed for our family and there was nothing we could do about it.

June's immediate reaction to the horrific event was a mental breakdown that led to her commitment at the Napa Mental Hospital. Her depression became so severe that Mom and Dad had to admit her to the San Francisco Mental Hospital. Apparently, doctors then believed that what June needed were drugs, more and more, stronger and stronger drugs. After weeks of regular, almost daily visits, and June's rapid deterioration to an almost zombie-like state, on what would be her final visit, Mother said to the doctors, "I'm taking my baby home."

Once at home, Mother bathed June, cooked for her, fed her, sat with her and talked with her, held her in her arms and cried with her, and took her to see movies in San Francisco. Mother, Grandma Roxie, Sister Lee and Dad nursed her back to health as best they could. Mother, years later, shared that she lived with the pain of guilt that she was responsible for what happened because she had asked June to go to the store that evening.

While physically she had recovered, June suffered from flashbacks and nightmares that made her want to be alone and then afraid to be by herself. She would cry and shake, and sometimes scream out loud at night saying she wanted to hide from everyone. In addition to having difficulty falling asleep, June had trouble concentrating, was often irritable, and had unpredictable, spontaneous outbursts of anger. The damage done to her body made it impossible for her to ever have children, even if she had wanted to. Psychologically, she felt vulnerable, detached, estranged, and alienated from other people. She was young and naturally wanted to go out, even at night for a walk or to a party but was too afraid. June displayed classic symptoms of Post-Traumatic Stress Disorder (PTSD).

My niece Faun was only three years old when it happened, when she was forced to witness her aunt being attacked. She, too, suffered mental and emotional trauma. She had witnessed June being a victim of intense physical violence, and I'm sure she suffered from PTSD as well, and understandably so.

———————◆———————

The music of 1960s (1968 and 1969 in particular) was arguably one of the country's greatest explosions of popular music since the 1920s. In 1968, Bonnie was eighteen and June fifteen and, since June was still at home, when she could, Bonnie took her to friends' houses where they would listen to songs like The Beatles' "Hey Jude," Otis Redding's "The Dock of the Bay," Hugh Masekela's "Grazing in the Grass," The Temptations' "I Wish It Would Rain," Jose Feliciano's "Light My Fire," Marvin Gaye and Tammi Terrell's "You're All I Need To Get By," and Aretha Franklin's "I Say A Little Prayer."

Bonnie, who was shorter and had darker skin than the rest of us girls, was also the visionary. In 1969, at nineteen, she dropped out of Merritt College, after that summer at Mills College, in Oakland. She especially liked the class with Cecil Brown who was quite the author: *The Life & Loves of Mr. Jiveass Nigger*, *I Stagolee* and *Stagolee Shot Billy* and *Dude, Where's My Black Studies Department*? He also taught Literature classes at U.C. Berkeley.

Bonnie studied Shakespeare with him and especially liked *Othello*. "I really liked Emilia, Desdemona's, sort of, big sister, who 'schools' the young Desdemona that there are some women who cheat on their husbands: 'There be some such, no question,' Emilia told her. Desdemona swears by the light of heaven she would never do such a thing; 'Not by this heavenly light!' Emilia tells her little sister, but 'might do it in the dark.' Then, Emilia tells her, basically, 'I think it is a man's fault if a woman cheats...the ills we do, their ills instruct us so.' Oh yeah, I like this sister, her spunk, and how it relates to my relationship with baby sister June."

We were all children of the '60s. We became teenagers when James Brown, Little Richard, Chuck Berry, Elvis Presley, Fats Domino, Little Willie John, The Shirelles, Etta James, Stevie Wonder, Kim Weston and Marvin Gaye, and Motown were popular. When June was twelve years old, she brought home a .45 of the Elvis Presley record "All Shook Up" and was surprised that Mother let her listen to it until she realized that Mother had been pacified by the song "Crying in the Chapel" (1965) on the "B" side of the record.

The '60s were also a time of social turmoil with the Vietnam War, demonstrations, riots, Apartheid, and assassinations. Medgar Evers was shot in the back while standing in the driveway of his home, John Kennedy was assassinated in Dallas, four little girls were bombed in a church in Birmingham, Malcolm X was assassinated by fellow Muslims, Martin Luther King was assassinated in Memphis, and Robert Kennedy was killed in Los Angeles.

FAIRYTALE

By 1969, Aaron, Fritz, Ruth, and I had families of our own—wives, husbands, children, and fulltime careers. Aaron was in Fukuoka, Japan playing professional baseball, Fritz was away at UCLA studying African History, Ruth was working as a keypunch operator for Folgers Coffee Company in San Francisco, and I had a career that I actually enjoyed as a legal secretary for the law offices of Metoyer and Sweeny in Oakland.

Chapter 5

HOUſTON OR BUſT

BY 1969, I WAS FOCUSED ON MY JOB AND MY DAUGHTER, WHILE MY sisters were making plans of their own. Bonnie was focused on a career in music and was confident that she could make it happen. Since I had to take care of my daughter, I was focused on my office job. It was not how I had envisioned my future, but I took comfort in the fact that I could support myself and Jada.

Meanwhile, Bonnie had convinced June to leave high school and join her in forming a singing group. June was only sixteen at the time, so she was willing to put her trust in Bonnie and give it a shot. "In 1969 when we formed the duo, *The Pointers – A Pair*," Bonnie said, "We tried to sing folk songs with Michael Takamatsu, who was also a guitarist, and then we'd do rhythm and blues covers in clubs because that was all the house bands could play. We played Al's House of Smiles on East 14th Street in Oakland, and The Lemington Hotel, and we played a cocktail party once for Belva Davis, the San Francisco news-woman, at her house. We opened the Wynn Hotel in Las Vegas. The two of us: June and I."

Bonnie had met Michael at a local grocery store in San Francisco. While waiting in line for the cashier, Bonnie said to Michael, who was wearing cowboy boots, a tie-dyed shirt, and bell bottoms with hair down to his butt, "You look like a musician or artist." Michael said, "I am." They became friends and Bonnie soon found herself in the exciting, creative community of musicians who were starting to gain notoriety in the San Francisco area.

One of the places where a lot of musicians and performing artists gathered was at the offices of Bill Graham and David Rubinson, which was directly across the street from the Fillmore West. On concert nights, David's office was like a second green room. Anybody from Jimi Hendrix to Dizzy Gillespie could be seen there on a concert night. Everybody in the music business came through at one time or another and Bonnie, Michael, and June were right there observing and learning and networking.

The electric, creative energy was infectious, and both of my sisters were addicted to the heady atmosphere. It wasn't all fun and games for them because they were making connections that they hoped would help further their fledgling singing career. Until they were able to get some paying gigs, they still had to support themselves.

Bonnie said, "These jobs were more for play than pay, and in 1970, to make some money, I tried topless dancing at Girls Galore on Telegraph Avenue in Oakland. I quit after a week. I couldn't stand it. It just wasn't my shtick; too many dirty old men. I just didn't like serving beer and having to sit and watch all those movies all night. It was just so low, so cheap. I wanted to be onstage, but that's *not* the way I wanted to be onstage. Before that, I was in the acid-rock age, and I was doing all those things—dropping acid and all—but in those days, it was fun, just trucking around the country."

Making way for the "perfect storm," David had relocated to San Francisco in 1969. Recall that fortuitously (or ironically), our family moved into a six-bedroom house on Oakland Avenue, and just down the street was a family named the Watsons. Their father was a minister and *The Watson Sisters* were four sisters who sang in church. Betty Watson was a good friend of Edwin and Tremaine Hawkins; she was the Director of the Northern California Youth Choir.

During that same time, June and Bonnie were looking for any work they could get where they could sing. They sang with a little pick-up garage band for an event at the Roosevelt Hotel in Oakland. They sang at Al's House of Smiles, also in Oakland, doing covers of Marvin Gaye and Tami Terrell: "Ain't No Mountain High Enough," and "Ain't Nothing Like the Real Thing."

Soon they worked their way up to a larger venue. In 1969, June and Bonnie would sing at Fillmore West with the Edwin Hawkins Singers, Northern California Youth Choir, on "Oh Happy Day."

Of course, they invited me to the show. I wasn't aware of the chaos going on backstage, but I had to go support my sisters. I also wanted to see how they were doing with their singing career. I wanted to see for myself. When I saw them perform, I cried because it was so emotional seeing them perform. I wanted to be up there on that stage with that choir, with Bonnie and June. It was amazing, absolutely amazing. So amazing that the very next day I quit my job and joined the Northern California Youth Choir, under the direction of Betty Watson and Edwin Hawkins.

Just after I joined, we were asked to travel with the choir. It was exciting for us, and it felt like I had made the right choice in giving up my job at the law firm. The three of us had one set of luggage to share. Mother had borrowed $300 for our trip, even giving us some spending cash just before we set off for our adventure. We were packed and ready to go when the phone rang. We got the news that the tour was cancelled just like that. I was learning real fast that show business is made up of constant ebbs and flows. That was the more difficult part for me, going from a stable nine-to-five to a life of hustling for gigs, but I was determined to make the best of it. Along with our work in the choir, the three of us were hanging out at the recording studio hoping for openings as background singers. We did have some initial success. "Oh Happy Day" by *The Edwin Hawkins Singers* became one of the top 100 singles of 1969, and Bonnie was in the choir of the original recording.

I was living back at the family home so that Jada could have a stable environment while I chased my dreams of singing with my sisters. One day, while walking home from the bus stop, there was this guy with a real nice maroon and black Thunderbird. He was from Texas. We became fast friends and I even joined him on a road trip from Oakland to Houston to meet his family. He promised that he could make things happen for us, and meeting his family convinced me that we should give it a shot.

When I got back from Houston, I told Bonnie and June that this guy knew people in Texas who could get us started in the music business. I had already done some of the background work to vet him as much as I could, and it felt like this might be my way of helping the group. The three of us agreed to pack up our things and hop in the Thunderbird with the man who could help us jump start our careers. We were buoyed with enthusiasm, singing in the car all the way to Texas, so much that we were hoarse by the time we arrived.

We got settled at his sister's house and then we were ready to get to work. He immediately took us to meet a man named Skipper Lee who had his own radio show, "The Skipper Lee Show." Skipper was going to introduce us to local movers and shakers. We went to his office full of enthusiasm only to be told that we needed to come back later. We were used to setbacks, so that was fine. We took it in stride. Still full of hope, we returned to his office to find the place was locked up, with no one around. Not a good start. Also, the sister we were staying with didn't want us to practice inside the apartment. We had to go sit in the Thunderbird if we wanted to rehearse. It was not what we'd had in mind.

However, we had already shipped all of our belongings to Houston by Greyhound, so we were dedicated to seeing this through. We did a show at the Greek Cat Night Club and Lounge. The show was great, but we knew that we needed to find a new place to stay. We'd met a girl at the Greek Cat, and we were desperate so we called her and she let us stay at her place in the fifth ward, a rough area of town.

Despite the meager, dirty accommodations, we were grateful, and it seemed like maybe this could work after all. Sure, there had been some problems, but that's the business. Then our "manager" started to become very demanding and controlling. That's when reality started to hit me.

These guys were not going to do anything for us. The man who made so many promises was nothing more than a shyster who really didn't know anyone in the music business. I really think his plan was to try and pimp out these three long-legged, attractive young women under the guise of "managing" us. I knew we had to get out of there.

First, I called Mother and she said, "I'll get my baby June home, but you and Bonnie are on your own!" As a result of hanging out at the recording studio in San Francisco, Bonnie had become friendly with Bruce Good and Jeff Cohen. We were desperate and didn't know where to turn. We had nothing to lose and Bonnie was always willing to take a risk, so she called those guys. They gave her the phone number of a man who would change our career and our lives—David Rubinson.

"When the call came," David says, "it was not 'hey we need three airline tickets,' not at all. They were in a really bad situation. I don't know if they were being held captive, or dominated or what, but it was not a good situation at all. This guy had kicked them out of a motel; they were living with someone they'd just met, in a roach-infested apartment; it was very bad, and what I did was the natural thing to do. I wasn't trying to be heroic, but helpful. Actually, they weren't calling *me*; I hardly knew them. Bonnie and June had just hung out around our studios and worked as backup singers on a demo for a songwriter I'd signed to the Fillmore Corporation's publishing company. They were calling Bruce and Jeff, who worked for me at the publishing company. They said they had been offered a contract on Zebra Records and should they sign? "Bruce and Jeff said, 'For God's sake don't sign anything.' They called back a day later and said things were falling apart. Bruce and Jeff gave them my phone number. They called, and I went down to the airport with my American Express card. They came to the office right off the plane, I got them into AF-TRA, and about a week later, we started recording.

"The funny thing about it was that, at the time of their call, my business with Bill Graham was falling apart, and I was in a rather tenuous financial situation myself: I was 28, I had a young son and a new daughter, and I was not sure what my next move would be. I had no company. I had no income. It was a very shaky time, a very scary time of my life. It's ironic because I was also in a funny place. I had discovered with Bill Graham that either you're his slave or his enemy.

"Still, I felt energized, bursting with creativity, intensity, and a sense of urgency. As someone might put it 'I was firing on all cylinders.' Perhaps my greatest weaknesses were impulsiveness, a quick fuse, and often insensitivity. Another thing some might say was that I am intensely loyal: when I got into a project it was all-consuming."

At the time, I wasn't aware of everything going on with David; in fact, I didn't know him personally, but I was so grateful that he had stepped in and helped us. It really showed us that not everyone was just talk. He sent us all airline tickets. He had never seen us before in his life, and we had never seen him. When we got to the Houston airport, this clown, the shyster, showed up demanding a ticket for himself. That was not going to happen.

When we got back to San Francisco, David put us to work right away singing backup for acts like Elvin Bishop, Cold Blood, Grace Slick, Sylvester, Boz Scaggs, and Esther Philips. We also did some jamming with Tower of Power. We did a show at The Boarding House in

San Francisco for $8.00 apiece. We were getting $25 per show with Elvin Bishop. It wasn't great money, but at least we were working!

I found out that our new friend, David Rubinson, had met Bill Graham because they co-produced the San Francisco Mime Troupe. Bill was the Business Manager of the Troupe. David produced a record called "Hey Joe," by Tim Rose, who was often compared to Ray Charles, Rod Stewart, and Joe Cocker. The song was one that Jimi Hendrix covered, and it became a #1 hit in San Francisco and several other cities. Bill saw David's name on the record and asked him, "Hey, did you produce this record?" David said, "yes" and Bill said, "How did you get this guy? He's a big hit out here." David had also produced albums for such acts as *Moby Grape* and the *Chambers Brothers* while still in New York.

The more I learned about David, the more confident I became that he would be able to help make our dreams a reality. Bonnie said, "David Rubinson saved my life. I wouldn't be who I am, The Pointer Sisters wouldn't be who they are, or where they are, without David Rubinson. He believed in me. He believed in us. He told me, 'You can do this.' And, I told him 'If you gave me a chance, I will not let you down.' I am grateful, truly grateful for what he did for me...for us."

We soon realized that David had his finger on the pulse of the music industry. "In 1970," David says, "the world for black entertainers and initiatives was circumscribed. But there were certain kinds of acts and performers who were successful and they, basically, fit certain molds. It was Motown or it was Rhythm and Blues in that very narrow definition, very limited creativity. A lot of backup singers, during this time, had grown up in the church and been gospel singers; still it was R&B—glittering gowns, straightened hair, and all that. Bonnie and June and Anita broke the mold. They were not your typical background singers; they were not brainwashed. They had a lot of initiative, a lot of confidence, and a good sense of themselves. So, they didn't dress or look or act anything like the stereotypical, circumscribed black girl backup singers. They weren't even close to that.

"I can recall in 1970, when they were doing backup for Sylvester. Can you imagine the impression this had on three girls of their age and background? Obviously, if you knew anything about Sylvester, the sisters were not in the mold of your typical backup singers. That's one of the most significant things I can say about them: they were *not in the mold."* To illustrate that unique and fierce individuality, just how out of the normal stereotype we were, David said, "They had a job as backup singers of Esther Phillips. They showed up for the show, at Ruthie's Inn in Oakland, part of the chitlin' circuit, archetypal, black R&B place, looking like they look. Esther was there in a purple florescent gown, hair straightened, nails done; and they come in wearing jeans with patches, one the red tongue of Mick Jagger sticking out, tie-dyed t-shirts, and regular shoes."

I remember that gig well. Esther was only paying us $10 each, per show, and she was not happy with how we looked. Bonnie said that, during the show, Esther sang the line, "Lord I got a cold feeling in my heart," then turned back and said to us "you black bitches are gonna be fired," then turned back to the audience and sang, "I said it's like ice around my heart," then back to us and said, "after this show, you bitches are gone."

Before the show, she had suggested that we take the money she paid us and go to an affordable department store, Lerner's, and buy dresses. We had different plans. We took that little money she was paying us and spent it on food. We weren't going back anyway. Besides, she was mean, even kicked my tape recorder, the one we used for practicing and rehearsing. It was not a good match to say the least.

"Once, Ruth came to our show and was sitting in the audience," Bonnie remembers. "Esther thought it was Anita and started scolding and cussing at her: 'What the hell you doin' sittin' out here? Damn it, we've got a show to do.' Well, she wasn't exactly Lena Horne, and maybe that was her problem."

In 1971, we continued to make the Fillmore West and David's office our home away from home. At the Fillmore, we saw acts like B.B. King, Jefferson Airplane, Tower of Power with Aretha Franklin, and Cold Blood. On concert nights, David's office was like a second green room.

David Rubinson had first heard Bonnie and June harmonizing on a demo tape of John Buckley that our friend Michael Takamatsu had played for him. "The demo," according to David, "was only pretty good; but what really got my attention were the background singers. At that time, it was June and Bonnie, The Pointers - A Pair."

After I joined the group, David became even more interested in our ability to harmonize and perform backup for any musical genre.

FAIRYTALE

At that time—when I was twenty-three, Bonnie was twenty-one, and June was eighteen—we began touring and performing backup vocals for many music acts that were breaking big all across the country. We moved into a third-floor Gough Street flat in San Francisco where we slept on mattresses on the floor.

As luck would have it, the apartment was within walking distance to Fillmore West and the office shared by David and Bill, and they were very supportive as we worked hard to build our reputation and our career. If we asked Bill for five dollars, he would give us fifty. If we asked for ten, he would give us one hundred. He told us not to tell anyone. He was such a kind and generous man, though he had a reputation of being strict. Fortunately, with us that was not the case.

We spent a lot of time in our apartment writing music and re-hearsing songs. We didn't just write song lyrics. The three of us also worked on commercials, anything to make money. Our first one was a jingle for Matthew Stereo in San Francisco that paid us $50! Next, was one for KSAN Radio. We wrote one for Colgate toothpaste that we hoped would be our big payday, but it was never used.

I was determined to write original music, and the three of us worked tirelessly, and June's talents were obvious from the start. David says, "June was very, very young. She, in a lot of ways, was the freest; she was the baby. And like a lot of 'babies' in large families, she had been able to do pretty much what she wants. She was also very funny, with a very ironic sense of humor. June could summarize an issue in about four words and get right to the heart of the matter. She was extremely intelligent and witty. She was also a great dancer. Her strongest asset, musically, was her freedom. She would take all kinds of chances. She had the highest-pitched voice, an incredibly high upper register with perfect pitch, and she had a very wide range. She had the largest range, vocally, of all the sisters.

"She also listened to a lot of different kinds of music and wasn't intimidated or limited by any type of music at all. She came of age in the late sixties, musically, and there were all kinds of music and social movements and protests going on. It was a new political scene: black people and young white and brown people were expressing different, rebellious, *break-the-mold* attitudes. No more status quo."

He was right. Bonnie and I were older so our determination was not as much of a surprise, but with June being so young, we were not sure if people would give her a chance; fortunately, David recognized her talents right away.

One of the main reasons that we had to keep going was our mother. She said, "I always showed my children I cared, that I was in their corner. I've always encouraged them in anything they were doing. Even in church I was behind them. Sometimes some of the church people discouraged them because they thought they were too loud and that was one of the reasons they gave up on gospel. I think they wanted to show those church people they could sing. They told us they were going to make us proud of them. Well, they got a proud mother. I hope they hurry up and get rich so I can retire."

Dad agreed, "Anything can happen to someone who puts her all into something. I was like that. Didn't believe in standing up there half-alive. I didn't preach a message until I felt that message down in my soul. The girls do that. And I love to see them come out. They trot out and when they're through, they trot off. I like that."

With their encouragement and David's support, we were ready to take on the world.

Chapter 6

BREAKING THE MOLD

N THE EARLY MONTHS OF 1971, JUNE, BONNIE, AND I TOURED WITH Elvin Bishop, sang background for Sylvester, and recorded with Taj Mahal, who was also kind enough to tell us that we should be getting paid not just for singing, but for writing and arranging background vocals as well. We were just happy to be working, so we didn't focus as much on the business side as we probably should have.

It didn't matter the venue; we would take work where we could find it. Bonnie remembers, "When we didn't have a recording session or stage show backup work to do, we would go to North Beach and sing for free at topless clubs. After the strippers took their intermissions, Anita, June, and I would hop up on stage and sing. We would sing a cappella, songs like: Aretha's 'Chain of Fools,' Carol King's 'You Got a Friend,' Johnnie Taylor's, 'Whose Making Love (to Your Old Lady)' —of course, we would change the line to 'your old man'—and Laura Nyro's 'Luckie' and 'Poverty Train.' We considered 'Poverty Train' our theme song."

Our willingness to take any gig we could find was paying off. We were getting more exposure and people in the music business were taking notice. It was while backing Elvin Bishop at the Whisky A Go-Go in Los Angeles that we heard a man named Jerry Wexler with Atlantic Records saw us, called David Rubinson, and said, "I've got to sign these girls." Once the details were worked out, Jerry sent us on the road to New Orleans and then back to San Francisco. Next, we got our own gig in London where we worked with The Dave Mason Band. It felt like our career as The Pointer Sisters was finally gaining some traction!

After we returned from Europe, our manager, Bill Graham, arranged a recording session for us with Atlantic Records in Jackson, Mississippi. David says, "We had started rehearsing, working on jazz and scat-singing, blues, country, and some R&B. They had all these songs that are on their first album: 'Cloudburst,' 'Shaky Flat Blues,' 'Wang Dang Doodle.' Atlantic didn't want to record it. They refused to record any of The Pointer Sisters' original material. Both Anita and Bonnie had written songs that are on the first album."

Not only had we toured around the US and England, now we were recording our own album! We flew to New Orleans where he hooked us up with Wardell Quezergue, the producer of the song "Mr. Big Stuff," by Gene Knight. We sang a few songs that we wanted to do for them, and they literally laughed in our faces, and said, "Black girls can't do songs like that." They wanted us to be more along the lines of Honey Cone and groups like that. Well, we didn't want to sound like Honey Cone. We wanted to be ourselves, but not everyone was able to see that we could cross-over into different music genres.

We loved groups like The Jacksons, Honey Cone, and singers like Marvin Gaye, Stevie Wonder, Aretha Franklin, Gladys Knight, Diana Ross, Smokey Robinson, Ashford and Simpson, the Philadelphia Sound, all of that; but we didn't want to imitate anybody. We had a country song, "Tulsa County," written by a friend of ours in Marin County. Atlantic flew us to Jackson, Mississippi to record; took us to dinner and put us up in a nice hotel. But they had changed that song so much we couldn't recognize it. It later became an R&B song even though it was written as a country song.

They gave us five songs to learn overnight, and then come back in the morning to record them. And we did. We signed with Atlantic Records and did our first single: "Don't Try to Take the Fifth on Me" in 1970. It may have even shown up on the charts, at number fifty-seven or something. For this, our first "record deal" we got a check for $1,000 to split among the three of us. Still, we were excited. It was a turning point.

When we returned to San Francisco and took the tape of our recording to David, he threw the tape across the room, and slung stuff off of his desk and screamed, "What the hell is that? You guys are not some typical black ghetto singers. What in the hell do they think they're doing? This is not what I wanted for you!" He had a fit.

He was really in a rage. Clearly, he did not want to put us in an R&B pigeonhole, which we appreciated.

"Instead," David remembers, "they recorded this stereotypical crap. The same old tired, *petrified mold* as ever existed." The "stereotypical crap" also included the song "Send Him Back." The company executives told us we needed to figure out what kind of music we wanted to sing because we can't sing everything. They said that because we were black, we have to sing R&B.

Bonnie said, "No, we don't. We can sing anything."

They said, "No, you gotta decide what kind of music you want to sing."

Bonnie wasn't backing down. "We've decided. We want to sing everything."

David, who produced our first five albums, describes Bonnie as "... completely rebellious. She is the spirit of assertiveness and self-confidence. She has an incredibly high energy and intense way of living. She lives life to the absolute limit, all the time. And, she would do anything, and say anything, and go anywhere...she didn't give a shit. She was very funny and very different from her sisters: physically, she was shorter and built differently than they were and she's of a darker hue. She had an incredible laugh, and she was also really wild. A very expressive, sexy, and alive presence, but would do just about anything. Bonnie was a troublemaker."

Talking about "trouble" and our growing notoriety for retro '40s attire, Bonnie said, "I had gotten into that in high school. See, I used to get kicked out of school because of the way I dressed, because it would be disrupting the classroom. I'd go to school with sequined blouses with shoulder pads, and big long coats. This dress thing has been wrongly interpreted. Some people thought we were trying to create nostalgia or re-creation of past times, but it was not that at all. We dressed this way years ago because we couldn't afford to dress better. We had been haunting thrift shops, and we sort of naturally developed a taste for '40s clothing."

David supported our evolving fashion style which began with Bonnie. He said, "She was wonderful in that way, because she was fearless. I'm sure it was Bonnie who said to her little sister, June, 'Let's go do this thing,' and not the other way around. It was Bonnie who was the spark, the catalyst, the one who wanted this music career to happen and would not be denied. It was Bonnie. And she was going to make it happen any way she could; even if it meant dragging her little sister over the bridge from Oakland to San Francisco. She got the auditions, the interviews, whatever it took to get into the business. She was the energizing force, very motivated and hungry."

Our experience in Mississippi was pivotal for David. "I could not believe what they had done. All the things we had talked about—being different, sounding different, and looking different—the producers ignored. I called Bill Graham and said, 'This is crap.' And he said, he didn't know what to do with them. I called Jerry and he said if the record the sisters recorded for Atlantic is a hit, then he and Graham would keep them. If it's not a hit, then I could have them. They put out 'Don't Try to Take the Fifth,' and it died. So, Bill Graham gave them the release, and so did Atlantic Records. They came downstairs to my office and we started putting together the material to go get them a record contract. This would be late 1971."

As we got more gigs, because of June's issues with depression and bipolarity, sometimes Bonnie and I would ask Ruth to fill in. When she did, she would make $50 to $100 dollars a night. Soon, after seeing the success we were enjoying, Ruth became a believer and wanted in, full-time. In addition, Mother insisted, and Ruth became the fourth Pointer Sister. Ruth had been working in San Francisco for the Folgers Coffee Company making $400 a month. Then she got blindsided by a bad decision. She was eighteen years old, got pregnant, and that turned everything around in her life. Her first high school boyfriend became the father of her first children: Faun, born in January 1965, and Malik, born in December 1965. She thought she was in love.

David said, "Ruth, at this time, was working as a keypunch operator. She had two children to support. She wasn't thinking about show business and wasn't going to be in show business. She was on a whole different path. If I can say this diplomatically, she wasn't breaking any *molds*. She was going to follow a very traditional, as it were, time-worn path. Joining her sisters saved Ruth's life. She was not going down a very good path at the time. They have an incredible natural harmony blend; the natural chords they sing, with no training, are not just 1-3-5-1 parallel harmonies. They hear chords that are not conventional. And in '72, when Ruth came in and sang a low A, I just about went out of my mind. She added a tremendous amount. Vocally, she added her fantastic range, because she has this amazing contralto voice."

So, in 1972, David officially left Bill Graham and formed his own company, David Rubinson and Friends. As part of their dissolution agreement, David got Tower of Power and The Pointer Sisters because, he said, "that's who I brought in. We started rehearsing, I went to Warner Brothers and they turned them down because they didn't sound like anybody else. I went to Columbia and Clive Davis, and he turned them down because they didn't sound like anybody else. They weren't the Honey Cone. Over and over when I went out with The Pointer Sisters or Herbie Hancock, people would say, 'We just don't know what to do with this.' It's an iconic statement with record companies: 'You know, we like you, but we just don't know what to do with this.'

"Bob Krasnow, a very, very aggressive, old-fashioned, real visionary record business guy had an independent label with some success. Bob said to me, 'You make good records: I want you to produce three artists a year for Blue Thumb Records. I had Herbie Hancock, Tower of Power, and now The Pointer Sisters. He gave me money, and he gave me a contract. I could produce and deliver anything I wanted. They would advance the recording costs. Bob Krasnow showed this great faith in me, giving me this opportunity to make whatever I wanted. Blue Thumb was now my label."

David says, "Krasnow knew the source material. Most of the people in the record business, including Clive Davis, had no idea who Lambert, Hendricks, and Ross were, or Muddy Waters for that matter. He knew when he heard June, Bonnie, Anita, and Ruth that they were something special. He would light up every time he heard them."

David was also producing and managing Herbie Hancock who was coming out with a new album, *Sextant*. David had learned of a cancellation by Ronnie Dyson ("When You Get Right Down to It" and "Just Don't Want to be Lonely") at the Troubadour in Los Angeles. He called Doug Weston, the owner, and suggested Herbie Hancock as a replacement. And why not this new group, The Pointer Sisters, to open the show? We were very excited, but there was an issue.

The four of us, The Pointer Sisters, did not have an act yet. David helped us come up with something fast. He says, "We had to put an act together. We went into a Studio Instrument Rental rehearsal studio in San Francisco, which has a stage, and we practiced 12½ hours a day for a week, preparing for The Troubadour. We went into the studio in rehearsal mid-1972 with all the songs that are on the first album. We recorded through January, February, and March of 1973. We finished recording in March of 1973. At this point, I was not only producing the record, I was managing The Pointer Sisters, which was something I had never done before.

"We never said, 'How are we going to make a pile of money?' I never recall having a meeting or even a talk with any one of The Pointer Sisters about what we can do to make a lot of money. They were just going for it, musically, artistically, and I was, too. I didn't care what the radio was playing or what X company wanted. In fact, one of those companies wanted me to tell Herbie Hancock to 'toe the line.' Now, how do you do that? We did talk about song selection, arrangements, who should sing lead, that sort of thing.

"Well, I was that way, and so were The Pointer Sisters. They came along when that was possible. My company with Bill Graham was breaking up. I was producing music outside the Bill Graham organization, trying to get on my feet again. Cold Blood was signed to the label I had with Bill. That was the company that was failing. I was working with groups that were outside the mold: Santana, Herbie, The Chambers Brothers.

"Like the Pointer Sisters, The Chambers Brothers came from a big family, and a preacher father; legend had it that the family walked from Mississippi to Los Angeles. The Chambers Brothers also *broke the mold*, like the sisters: they wrote their own music; they didn't do choreography, and they dressed in outrageous, un-matching outfits, and they sang their own way, and they were successful. Part of the reason for that success was their difference."

As the Pointer Sisters, we also created something completely unique. We were willing to take chances because at that point, we had nothing to lose. We had already been told we shouldn't do certain types of songs, and that wasn't what we wanted. It was apparent to us that we had to do things our way and make sure folks didn't try to mold us after other groups. We didn't want to imitate anyone else. We wanted them to do their thing, and we wanted to do ours. Our rebellious nature probably had a lot to do with growing up in the

San Francisco area at the time because the atmosphere was all about being yourself and taking chances.

Our look evolved from Bonnie's high school experimentation through excursions at local thrift shops where we bought '40s-style dresses, and feather boas. We borrowed a clothes rack from David's office and used that to hold all of our stage outfits. David set up a dress rehearsal for us at Bimbo's, a nightclub in San Francisco. This would be the very first time The Pointer Sisters performed our stage act. We had already built a large gay following due to singing background vocals for Sylvester and we were anxious to see how others responded to our act.

There was a group that David was considering for his label who he invited to join us in the show; however, that didn't go as planned. After we took our place on stage, the other band came out in costumes that alarmingly resembled Ku Klux Klan uniforms with pointed hoods and all. I wasn't sure what was happening, but we all had heightened awareness of Civil Rights thanks to Fritz, so this was outrageous. Fortunately for us, David was livid and had them removed from the stage. He later refused to work with them.

Keep in mind that we were dressed in Billie Holiday, '40s attire. And there's all that connection to the song "Strange Fruit" and that whole period of lynching. I was so scared, terrified. I did not look back toward the band. I was so nervous; I didn't know what to do but sing. We were hoarse from 13-hour-a-day rehearsals, for a week, but this was something we had to do. The Klan, in the band, on the first night of our professional act, can you imagine? It chills me to the bone.

Bonnie was less affected by the bizarre outfits. "You know, I really didn't give a damn what the backup band was wearing; that's what they were, the backup band. The Klan was backing up this black group, these black women. We were in front. They were our backup band. We were the headliners. I didn't give a damn if they were wearing nothing at all…play the fucking song and play it right. Shit, I'll snatch those hoods off their damn faces. It was like four Billie Holidays with a KKK backup band. Now can you see that, four Billie Holidays and a Ku Klux Klan backup band? They probably did it thinking we would mess up, that we would be scared, so scared we would fail. But it didn't work. Their little Halloween bullshit caper failed. Maybe they thought it was funny. Well, we did our show, and they got fired."

David went down to Los Angeles and found a Public Relations firm, Gibson and Stromberg, a rock and roll firm. They had the connections, worked with a lot of industry people and they got the people out to The Troubadour to see us. He had also taken the album to KSAN radio, and they latched onto it and played it non-stop. By the time we got to L.A., the buzz about "The Sisters" was growing. In May 1973, for a week, The Pointer Sisters opened for Herbie Hancock, and our first album came out the same month. The stars were aligning for us and everything seemed like it was falling into place as far as our career was concerned.

David was very happy with the attention we were receiving. "If ever there were a 'break through' performance in American music history, this was it." Our gig at The Troubadour in Los Angeles lasted a week, with three shows on the weekend. Combined with the radio play and our growing fan base, our shows were nothing short of electrifying. It was absolutely unbelievable. It seemed everybody in L.A. caught the buzz. There were lines around the block every night. A diverse, eclectic audience if ever there was one. We fed off that energy and channeled it into our performances, getting standing ovations every night.

I couldn't believe that all of our hard work was finally paying off. It felt amazing and that success only helped to bond us as not only sisters, but as The Pointer Sisters. We all understood that what we had created was powerful. The sky was the limit and our future was up to us. We needed to take care of our career, make smart decisions, and keep a level head. That was not easy to do because in show business, once that momentum begins, it's not easy to slow down and take stock of what is happening. It's much easier to just go with the flow and ride the wave. However, this was going to be our livelihood and the way I would support my daughter, so it needed to be a serious venture. We were adults now, not sisters singing in Daddy's church choir. We were ready to take on the world.

Following our triumphant headliner debut, we returned to San Francisco to play the Great American Music Hall, again opening for Herbie Hancock who was also gaining in popularity. Herbie also realized that with The Pointers Sisters on the bill, he was bound to gain new followers. David hoped we would complement each other. He says, "Herbie's life was also changed by that week with The Pointer Sisters. He saw what was going on with The Sisters and said, 'Ah-ha, I'll have some of that, thanks very much; I'll have two orders of that please.' He got rid of his band, changed completely and went into the studio with a whole different direction. He did the *Headhunters* album, one of the best-selling jazz albums in history. Hancock later remarked, 'The beauty of life is to be outside the box, so that the box doesn't exist...to limit a human being to one mode of expression is really a crime.'"

After the Great American Music Hall, we were official headliners, proving that we could bring in a crowd. Our next gig was a week at The Boarding House in San Francisco. The Boarding House was important because it was the place where Bette Midler had broken all kinds of attendance records with lines around the block. Then we came along and attracted an even bigger audience so we had high hopes that our show would also be successful. We just had no idea how well it was going to be received.

As predicted, it was an incredible week. We had a hard time believing what was happening. At every show, people were working hard to get in, many being turned away, lines winding down the street. It was insane. People were begging for tickets. Lines formed at one o'clock in the morning, with people hoping to ensure they would be allowed into the next show. David was very proud of us and even invited Bill Graham to attend, and there he was, third row center, watching us give the performance of our lives.

We strolled onto the stage, draped our feather boas and wraps on the borrowed coat rack, then stood in line in our thrift shop original lavender, red, yellow, and blue silk dresses. We would hold our poses as the crowd went wild, the air building with anticipation. It was time for us to perform, to deliver as folks expected. Word had spread that The Pointer Sisters were the hottest and most unique group around, and we had to make sure not to disappoint.

Once the applause died down, we broke into Jon Hendrick's "Cloudburst," singing in unison and milking the crowd, then we'd segue into "Jada" a song written about my daughter. We were serving echoes and memories of The Andrews Sisters with a modern twist, and people loved it. Then we would shift to an upbeat rock song like "Yes, We Can (Can)" and move to blues with "Wang Dang Doodle."

We transitioned quickly from one song to the next. The audience went wild when they realized they had no idea what was coming at them. They barely had time to recover from an R&B song when we hit them with a blues tune. It was an amazing transference of energy and excitement.

Long and lean, we played up our sexuality and the sight of four pretty sisters performing together. All of our practice and backup singing and gigs at strip clubs had paid off. We knew how to play to the audience, and we became more polished with each show. It's all about timing in the entertainment industry and fortunately for us, there was a void in vocal groups that focused on harmonies. Being sisters only added to our allure and made people want to come out and see what we were like at a live show.

The next show we did was at the Circle Star Theater in San Carlos, California, a gigantic theater-in-the-round. It was the first big concert, and *The San Francisco Chronicle* sent Jon Hendricks to review it. Jon Hendricks, of the singing trio Lambert, Hendricks, and Ross, a very important performer and composer in jazz music, was their resident jazz critic. He was renowned for putting lyrics to well-known jazz instrumentals by Count Basie, Horace Silver, and Eddie Jefferson, and turning them into exceptional achievements of musical art. As with the Boarding House show, we opened the show with "Cloudburst" which is a song he wrote, and we were told it was very emotional for Jon.

At the end of the show, he came backstage and told us how much it affected him. We felt so good because we were showing the industry that we could back up what we promised we could do. We were able to sing songs that we liked, and people were responding. It felt good to prove to those who kept saying "we don't know what to do with you" that we were capable of R&B and so much more. Hopefully those naysayers would think twice before judging other groups so quickly. For us, on that night, *we broke the mold.*

Reviews of our show were equally flattering and helped to confirm our status as headliners who were making big waves in the music industry. We brought in diverse crowds that came to see and hear "those foxy girls from Oakland." People responded to our story of sisters who, after four years of backup singing and second-billing club dates, had finally arrived on our own terms. They responded overwhelmingly when we transitioned easily between genres like jazz, rock, gospel, R&B, and even "country/western." We were also happy that our success reflected well on David, and we had proved to him, like Bonnie promised in Houston, that we would make him proud, that he wouldn't be sorry if he took a chance on us.

Occasionally, June could not or would not make some tour and performance dates. I was simply amazed that with her recent traumatic past, she could perform with such energy and passion and become the professional that she had become, so I understood when she sometimes didn't feel up to it. There was no high school campus life or college life for June: no dating, no sporting events, no senior prom. She went right into the working world, so it had to be difficult for her.

Not yet twenty-one, she sang with power, with the deep conviction and joy of a rigorous spiritual household. Her voice and stage performance were described as "unrestrained, exuberant, soulful, wicked, wild, and truthful." All one has to do is listen to her incredibly soaring soprano, at eighteen years old, singing "Cloudburst" or "Sugar" or "Pains and Tears" on our first album. And like with Minnie Ripperton you would ask yourself, "How does she get that high and stay in harmony?" Next thing you know, on "Naked Foot" she'd growl like Louis Armstrong.

That first album, *The Pointer Sisters* (1973), went gold. In those days, a gold album meant something. Nowadays, you have to be triple platinum or better, but back then, a gold album was really remarkable, especially a first album. The hit single was "Yes We Can (Can)" written by Allen Toussaint, a great lyricist. We found that song on a Lee Dorsey album and took it to David and told him, "This is the kind of song we want to sing." It had been on an album of Dorsey's years ago and had such a great message.

The song I wrote, "Jada," was also on this first album. It was just a fun little song. I didn't think much about it, but we would play around with it backstage. David heard us singing it, a cappella, liked it and put it on the album. Bonnie and I also wrote the song "Sugar" for that first album. We were living in Pleasanton at the time. We were enjoying a little herb, one day, and noticed our next-door neighbor in full police uniform. We moved the next month. David was willing to take a chance on us, and we didn't want to mess that up by getting into any trouble.

BREAKING THE MOLD

That first album, *The Pointer Sisters*, was recorded by genius engineer Fred Catero in early 1973. By June it had sold over 500,000 units (Gold). It hit the *Billboard* Charts on June 23, and black radio had still not touched it. They didn't play anything until the single "Yes We Can (Can)" released in July was on the *Billboard* Charts in August. It just wasn't the *kind* of music they were playing. They were playing Honey Cone, The Jackson Five, and The Supremes. We were something new and different.

We were not only known for our voices and the stage performances, but our fashion was becoming increasingly popular. We certainly didn't have a wardrobe assistant, and just wore the antique clothes that were now a part of our everyday style. They were clothes we used to play grown-up in as children, things we found in old trunks at relatives' houses.

David Rubinson said, "That dress. The one you wore the other night to the party. That dress. That's the one we want for your first album cover." I couldn't believe it. I was thinking, "I wear that dress all the time, or something similar." So, on that first album cover, that is my dress; the shoes are from London, and the hats we have on came from Mother's church friends, and the fur I have on is from Sister Tires. We searched attics and basements for the clothes we wore in that first photo shoot, for that first album cover. We had no idea of the impact it would have.

Jazz was a passion of David's. "I gave them Lambert, Hendricks, and Ross and said, 'Go learn this,'" he recalls. "I had this treasure trove of material that was *mold-breaking* material, that I couldn't get people to record. 'Yes, We Can (Can)' was a song I tried to get Lydia Pense (*Cold Blood*) to record, but she wouldn't do it. But The Pointer Sisters *broke the mold* again because they wrote their own songs, and many black women in the 1970s did not write their own songs."

Released in 1973, *The Pointer Sisters* was unlike any other album of its time. From straight-ahead R&B (Allen Toussaint's "Yes, We Can (Can)") and scat-jazz (Jon Hendricks' "Cloudburst") to funk jams (like Wilton Felder's "That's How I Feel") to blues-rock (Willie Dixon's "Wang Dang Doodle") and their own self-penned jazz compositions ("Jada" and "Sugar"), *The Pointer Sisters* embraced as many styles as possible, simply because we could sing skillfully, honestly, and with commitment.

FAIRYTALE

Public reception was amazing. "Yes, We Can (Can)" landed at #11 on the pop charts and "Wang Dang Doodle" landed at #24 on the R&B charts. David used some of the most talented musicians in the business—Drums: Gaylord Birch and Ed Marshall; Guitar: Willie Fulton; Bass: Ron McClure and Dexter C. Plates; and Piano: Tom Salisbury and Norman Landsberg. The backing band on "Wang Dang Doodle" was The Hoodoo Rhythm Devils.

David had a cohesive vision. "The way I am is that I do what I like and then try to make it commercial. I don't take things that are already finished and package them. I loved, as Frost said, to 'take the road less traveled.' Being another girl singing group did not interest me. It didn't interest them, either. So, I listened to the songs they had written: 'Jada,' and 'Sugar,' both on the first album, and others; and I introduced them to what I liked: Lambert, Hendricks, and Ross, King Pleasure, and Eddie Jefferson." Clearly, David had the foresight, insight, courage, and fortitude to accept and encourage our imagination and creativity: to take and use songs we had composed as a part of our first album. David even recognized and encouraged my love of singing country/western music.

Like I said, this business is all about timing. During one of our early shows, Jeff Wall, the husband of singer Helen Reddy, was in the audience. Helen Reddy had just gotten a summer replacement show taking the place of *The Flip Wilson Show*. Jeff saw us and apparently relayed to Helen, "You have to have these girls on the show." We not only did her show, we recorded with her and went on the road with her, even to Hawaii. Then we ended up going on to appear on many TV variety shows that were popular at the time: *The Carol Burnett Show, The Flip Wilson Show, Johnny Carson, The Mike Douglas Show, American Bandstand, The Midnight Special*. Those appearances were great for exposure and generating even more publicity.

Free from the pigeonhole of conventionally molded R&B female vocal groups, we had unintentionally created a cultural shift in clothing and musical style. It was uninhibited, eclectic, and free. We had maintained our integrity and our individuality while creating a new, collective identity. We were also unique because there was not one lead singer. In sisterly fashion, we took turns singing lead on songs that best suited each of our voices. It was a collaborative venture from the beginning.

BREAKING THE MOLD

We went on a club tour with Dick Gregory, a concert tour with the band Chicago, did television specials, and performed in concerts and clubs before starting work on our second album. That fall, June turned 20, and a European tour was planned for January 15 to February 3, 1974. The expected highlight of this trip was an appearance at the important MIDEM (International Record and Music Publishing Market) convention in Cannes, leading to a slot on a Eurovision network television special, which an estimated 100 million people would see. This European trip was our first real promotional tour. That usually means the goal is to get exposure even if it ends up losing money. We played London, Amsterdam, Paris, Cannes, and Bremen, Germany. David was there with us as well as a wardrobe woman, tech and crew, and musicians: Tom Salisbury (pianist and musical director), Gaylord Birch (drums) and John Neumann (bass) rounded out the group.

The crucial business of the tour was divided into three key performances: A private promotional party in London, the MIDEM concert in Cannes, and a public concert in London. We first performed in London, at the opening of the Rainbow Room of the world-famous trendy fashion palace called Biba's. It was, apparently, the toughest kind of invited audience, well-oiled journalists and blasé musicians. Rod Stewart was there, as was the Faces' Ron Wood, the Kinks' Ray Davies, Traffic's Jim Capaldi, and Neil Sedaka.

But most importantly, Annie Ross was there. The fabled lady, indisputably one of the greatest of jazz singers, co-author of "Twisted" (recorded by both Joni Mitchell and Bette Midler), cleaned up from a heroin habit which ruined Lambert, Hendricks, and Ross. Now active in English musical theater and clubs, Annie Ross was there at the invitation of David to see what she had spawned.

June was especially nervous that night, but from the moment she began singing "Cloudburst," handling the triple-tonguing tempos with ease, trading scat solos with Bonnie, Ruth, and me, like bebop trumpeters and saxophonists, everything was all right. We were on our way, again. Scheduled to do only three or four songs, we did five and we were called back for an encore by a sincere display of howls and shrieks. We chose "Little Pony," another song associated with Lambert, Hendricks, and Ross, and dedicated it to Annie. She could not help but get emotional.

There were different challenges: a middle-aged and very square audience at the MIDEM "Gala" and a very youthful, hip and demanding, and again extremely diverse, crowd at London's Victoria Palace, but we seemed to move among the different groups with ease. We stayed true to our act despite the audience, sauntering onstage, doffing our seedy wraps onto our traveling coat rack to reveal glittery evening gowns.

We started off with some playful banter with the audience. "We like old songs, old clothes, and old men...young men, too." Then we launched into our four-song set which included "Cloudburst," "Jada," "Wang Dang Doodle," and "Old Songs." Our talented accompanists were impeccable. We also had special guest, Wah Wah Watson, who was a celebrated guitarist working with folks like Quincy Jones and Barry White. He was known for his ability to use a wah-wah pedal to create amazing, unique sounds.

We also integrated some basic choreography, nothing too precise because we each liked to give the moves our own twist, to show that we were a unified group but with different personalities. Just like the way we traded off lead vocals, our goal was to make sure each of us got to shine. Then when we came together with tight harmonies, it just blew people away. We just wanted the audience to feel good, and that night, everything came together perfectly.

One of the British record producers who saw us at MIDEM said, "They have the greatest potential of any act I've ever seen." Stevie Wonder, who was making his first public appearance at MIDEM since his near-fatal accident, sang a song he wrote for us. It was at a rehearsal, and he was accompanied only by his own piano. It was a magic moment as we clustered around while he sang "Sleeping Alone," a funky and soulful song that we would eventually record. David took us and Stevie to spend a delightful afternoon shopping together in the medieval village of St. Paul.

It didn't require intimate knowledge of the French language to translate the headlines of the *Nice-Matin* "Le triomphe des *Pointer Sisters*." Both in concert performance at the Palais des Festivals and in print, we were celebrated that evening and our performance was transmitted to as many as 100,000,000 people on the Eurovision television network. The article in the local newspaper was primarily devoted to a story about The Pointer Sisters, with mentions of Montand, and the remaining six acts, including Stevie Wonder in his first concert appearance since his automobile accident the previous summer. The overwhelming reaction we received was no surprise to our solid fan base in the Bay Area, but we all enjoyed the result of our hard work. It felt amazing to watch others discovering our group and loving what we were all about. During that show, we learned that our music appealed to a broad demographic. It went far beyond our devoted San Francisco fans. At this performance, we were playing for a largely white audience primarily made up of men in the music industry, always a tough crowd!

It seemed that after our show, the audience had had its fill. They typically attend these events in search of the hottest new groups, those on the verge of exploding into the world of music, especially the fast-growing and lucrative pop genre. Apparently, what they saw in us was a group that could effortlessly cross genres. In our show, we'd go from jazz to R&B to pop with ease. The way we delivered the songs, our look, our stage presence, it all worked together and convinced audiences to find joy in the music, no matter what genre they usually listened to. Our set was so successful, that we saw several people walking out when Stevie Wonder took the stage. He was already a known commodity, and many were convinced they'd just seen the next big thing...and they had! I was elated by our success, but I also enjoyed the fact that Stevie and I became friends. He even called me later to sing "Happy Birthday" to me.

Then it was back to the States. We sang "Bei Mir Bist Du Schoen" on the Pat Boone television special *One More Time* with Patti Andrews, a singing sister from another generation. We talked excitedly about our forties-inspired hairstyles and clothes. We had an instant connection with Patti because she said we were bringing back fashions that she had pioneered 30 years prior!

It felt like The Pointer Sisters were here to stay.

Chapter 7

STEAM HEAT

BEFORE WE KNEW IT, WE WERE HIRED FOR OUR FIRST MAJOR appearance. It was to open for Paul Anka at the $60 million Caesars Palace hotel and casino in Las Vegas. The suites were complimentary, the house orchestra was excellent, and the sound system in the 1,200-seat main showroom was first-class. When we arrived, we couldn't believe how beautiful it was, and the billing was impressive: THE POINTER SISTERS in letters the size of a small person emblazoned right below PAUL ANKA on the marquee.

We were going to be paid $100,000 for the two-week gig. Dad had not made that much in 22 years as a pastor. However, our excitement faded when the opening-night audience greeted us with near hostility. The headliner, Paul Anka, came out and tried to help. He was yelling at the audience, trying to convince them to give us a chance. "They are the most exciting new act I've seen in years!" The problem was that the audience had come to see *him,* Paul Anka. They had no idea who we were.

There was also a personal crisis that threw off the act. The day we were to open, June would not come out of her hotel room. Physically and emotionally exhausted following the almost month of touring in Europe, she locked herself in her room and would not come out; not even after we sent for Mother who was flown down to plead with her. She would not make the opening curtain.

Suddenly, songs had to be dropped, choreography adjusted, arrangements rearranged. And the show that remained, according to one critic, "was more suited to a small club stage than the cavern that is the Circus Maximus." It was difficult for everyone because we already knew the crowd was not welcoming and then we had to hastily change the show at the last minute. It was not the recipe for success, especially for a group just starting out.

With a busload of Blue Thumb executives and selected press on hand, rumors began to circulate that June was ill, had mononucleosis, or had gone bananas. Gibson & Stromberg, our publicists, would later attribute her absence to a nervous breakdown. The truth was, after a thorough examination, that she was suffering physical and mental exhaustion from the chaotic three weeks in Europe.

David remembered it well. "Sometimes, it seemed that the story was about June, and how she didn't show up, etc. But this was not the deeper story. We were all exhausted, but the Caesar's engagement was the biggest payday we had ever had. We really needed the money. When we arrived at the hotel the morning of the day before the opening, our hotel rooms were not ready! Not even the special VIP suites for the sisters. One of the many mistakes I made that week that caused some of the problems. We all had to sit in the lobby for a few hours. In my inexperience, I didn't realize that the talent-booking department and GM of the hotel could have straightened it out in minutes, which they ultimately did, but it left us even more tired.

"I had hired a Broadway choreographer for 'Steam Heat'— especially for the Vegas crowd. We scheduled a rehearsal for the night of our arrival to make sure the song would be ready for the next night. I underestimated how very exhausted June was. I was insensitive to her fragility. The others were real 'troupers' and would work their way through just about anything—but June was much frailer, physically and emotionally. In my desire to make the show great, I pushed them too hard, and June finally cracked and walked out, loudly. My next mistake was to blame her and not empathize with her and understand her history (of which I was unaware).

"I went to her room, and she was in bad shape. She had what was sometimes called a 'breakdown' — curled up in her bed, uncommunicative. Her sisters came to see her as well, but she was not reachable. We decided to call their mom, who flew to Vegas immediately. June was taken by ambulance to the airport, and Mrs. Pointer took her back with her to Oakland where she was admitted to the hospital. I now realize how fragile she was and had always been, and also how much responsibility I must take for her breakdown in Vegas. For me, this story was not just about June, but also about my ambition and insensitivity and tragic lack of empathy."

David was trying to handle the situation the best way he knew how. I'm sure it was overwhelming for him, with all of us hoping this was our big break; to see it falling apart was difficult. The three of us went onstage and did our best, but it wasn't what we'd planned. Paul Anka was not happy with our performance either, but we did make changes, as shows often do, and it improved dramatically during our engagement there; but apparently David was dealing with other issues.

David said, "I was called for a meeting in the talent manager's office. I was basically surrounded. The boss turns to his assistant: 'Frank, when we went to see these girls in Los Angeles, how many girls were there?' Frank, holding up four fingers, says 'Four...definitely four.' 'And Frank, did you see the show last night?' 'Oh yeah.' 'Well, how many girls were on the stage? Three.' Holding up three fingers, 'Definitely three. Well,' — he said finally addressing me, 'we paid for four, but we got three. What are we going to do about it?'

"All I could say in reply was, 'I'm really sorry, but there's nothing we can do. The youngest girl got very ill last night and was taken by ambulance to the airport, and she's in the hospital now.' And that was it. They later went back and had very successful appearances there."

Of course, as her family, we knew that June was probably the weakest one of us. She hadn't been the same since the attack. We didn't know if she would ever be over it. What does that mean, when people say, "Get over it," or "Move on?" How the hell do you do that? I was amazed that she was able to do as much as she did.

I guess because I was older, I felt protective of the group and my sisters. David often called me the rational and reasonable one. He said I was the most even-tempered and the self-appointed mother hen of the group. He's probably right about that because I felt a natural instinct to help June and the others whenever I could. I moved in to try and handle most of our business and financial matters and also acted as spokesperson for the group. I suppose it was an extension of my work ethic. Whether at the law firm or in a singing group, I liked to have things orderly and professional.

STEAM HEAT

A few weeks after our shaky Vegas performance, on April 21, 1974, we were playing at the San Francisco Opera House. June was fully rested and back with the group. I felt like we were whole again, and we were all filled with positivity. I'm not sure if the craziness at Caesar's hurt our career or helped it because suddenly, it seemed, The Pointer Sisters were one of the hottest properties in the United States entertainment business. It's difficult to explain, but we could just feel the energy that night before the show. Everything was falling into place, and it felt even sweeter because June was back where she belonged.

Bill Graham and David were building up the show as an event not to be missed, and the public was responding. BILL GRAHAM PRESENTS: THE POINTER SISTERS – LIVE AT SAN FRANCISCO MEMORIAL OPERA HOUSE – Sunday, April 21, 1974 8:00 p.m., Black Tie Optional. With Thomas E. Salisbury, Conductor and Music Director: And Gaylord Birch, drums and John Neumann, bass – Special Overture Composed by Thomas E. Salisbury.

Bonnie, June, Ruth and I put on one of our best shows up to that date. We were in our '40s outfits and we were filled with non-stop energy. Our performance was on point, the orchestra was amazing, the audience went wild, and that energy just propelled us to new heights. It was a pivotal performance for us, and we knew that it could make or break us. Fortunately, it was probably the turning point in our career, the defining moment where we knew our group was solidified and we were doing what preparation and opportunity intended and rewarded.

From the time the first limousine full of concert-goers pulled up with a champagne-sipping group of men in formal attire and women in lace, fur, and feathers, it was apparent that the night had a character of its own. Two decisions—to use the Opera House and to promote "black tie optional"—paid off. The show started late because the crowd came to see and be seen. It was difficult to get them all seated. This was San Francisco. At 8:20, the lobby parade was finally over and the huge gold curtain rose majestically to the ornately designed ceiling, revealing a magnificent, full orchestra of 15 violins, 3 cellos, a bass, a dozen horns—6 trumpets and 6 trombones—piano, drums, guitar, and percussion.

FAIRYTALE

Led by pianist Tom Salisbury, our wizard pianist, arranger, conductor, and music director resplendent in tuxedo and ruffles, he assumed the spot where Toscanini once stood and gave the downbeat for an original overture of his own composition. Salisbury, who played like Fats Waller, Art Tatum, or Horace Silver at the drop of a lyric, was joined by Gaylord Birch on drums, John Newmann on bass, and Chris Michie on guitar.

Then the stage went dark and anticipation rose in the great old building for the return of their prodigal daughters. Everyone knew what was coming. Everyone was ready: their daughters, their sisters, nieces, childhood friends were coming home as certified stars.

A spotlight hit stage left and Bonnie, regal in all white, strode purposefully forth, deposited her wrap on the ancient coat hanger (which was as much a part of the act as "Cloudburst"), and stood happily buffeted by a storm of applause. Next, I walked out with June and Ruth, and we whipped into Dizzy Gillespie's "Salt Peanuts" from our recent Blue Thumb album *That's a Plenty*. When we first got the song, all we had were the two words "salt peanuts." It was Jeffrey Cohen and Bruce Good who wrote the lyrics. They really did an incredible job and audiences always responded to it enthusiastically. That night was no exception.

As the show continued, there was dancing in the aisles and even in the box seat area. Being San Francisco, the crowd was a wonderful mix of new straight fans and plenty of our gay followers. It was the perfect combination. At one point, we were wailing "Steam Heat," the band was blowing it up, and the gays were screaming with delight!

In our repertoire that night, we performed thirteen songs including a rare treat, the Everly Brothers' "Let It Be Me" which had not yet been recorded. We wanted to make sure our performance of that song was flawless, each of us taking a solo spot. Next, Bonnie brought Paul Webster and Sonny Burke's "Black Coffee" under mellow and sensuous control. Then we did "Shaky Flat Blues" about our first little run-down apartment in San Francisco. It was written by me, June, and Bonnie with June singing lead.

We were the first contemporary act to play that Opera House, and no detail was spared. They had cigarette girls with the little pillbox hats going through the audience to add to the atmosphere. *San Francisco Chronicle* writer John Wasserman called the concert at

San Francisco's War Memorial Opera House, "simply one of the great music events in San Francisco history...the vibes, you should pardon the expression, were dizzyingly high, warm, expectant, and just plain good."

After a few stops and starts, we were finally on our way.

Chapter 8

BROWN BABIES

A
S THE SISTER WHO WAS MOST FOCUSED ON THE BUSINESS SIDE, I was learning a lot about how to appeal to various types of audiences. I was careful to take note of what was working and more importantly, what wasn't. Our early gigs were a perfect training ground and truly helped us make the adjustments necessary to ensure that we were reaching our audience. It was much different from singing back in Daddy's church. Doing this professionally meant there were so many more components that we had to be aware of, especially how we were coming across to the audience. It was literal on-the-job training, and the truth was that we just wanted to sing...together.

Before going back into the studio, David had arranged for us to play a nostalgic "Back to the Forties" evening at the famous Roseland Ballroom in New York City. It was designed and decorated like a 1940s speakeasy, with period memorabilia and high style, including white tablecloths and candles. It was an absolutely fabulous event. I felt we had gone back in time.

We arrived for the sound check at around 3:00 that day and went incognito because we were starting to get recognized everywhere that we went. While that caught us off-guard, I knew it was a sign that we were on the right track. David was a genius at orchestrating events, and this was no exception. After the sound check, we waited in our dressing rooms until the 8:00 show. When it was time to get ready, we slipped into our nostalgic outfits because they fit with the evening, and audiences really responded to that look. At 7:30, David had us slip out the back door, hop into an awaiting limo and drive around the block to the entrance where fans and paparazzi had gathered. It reminded me of the show at the San Francisco Opera House:

concert-goers arriving in vintage limousines wearing stylish 1940s garb.

At an event like that, we had to make an entrance and that's what we did. We pulled up in the white Rolls Royce and emerged in colorful dresses, feather boas, and hats onto the red carpet. We were immediately mobbed by fans, our eyes adjusting to the flashbulbs bursting in front of us. It was such a surreal moment, a culmination of all our hard work. I looked around and was happy to see that as usual our crowd was quite diverse. There were some older black people likely anxious to see Louis Jordan, the opening act. Then there were young black and white fans, and our ever-devoted gay following. It was everything I could have imagined.

In attendance were the who's who of New York and beyond, including the Rockefellers, the Kennedys, the Clintons, Liza Minnelli, and Stevie Wonder. I was so excited to see Stevie again after the show in Europe. Our performance went off without a hitch and the audience responded with pure enthusiasm. Playing that prestigious venue after our triumphant tour overseas only helped to confirm what I was now realizing. Dreams really can come true.

I returned to my condo in Sausalito, California, at 5 Marie Street (the address was always easy for me to remember since my middle name is Marie). The next thing I know, David was calling me from his office in San Francisco. He said, "Stevie Wonder is here, and would like to do some writing with us. Can you come over?"

I played it cool. "Sure," I said, trying not to scream. I was in a trance. I just love Stevie. When he sings "My Cherie Amour!" Oh, I love that song, and used to hug that record and imagine him holding me. Of course, I broke every speed limit driving across the Golden Gate Bridge to San Francisco, down Lombard to Van Ness to David's Market Street office. I couldn't believe how quickly our career was moving. I was 22, single, a member of a hot new group, and now working with Stevie Wonder! I was elated!

In one of David's offices, Stevie and I started writing the song "Sleeping Alone" and, after some time, Stevie, Bonnie, and I did a run-through over at Wally Heider Studios. That evening, my dream became reality when Stevie came to visit me in Sausalito. He brought a bottle of Blue Nun, his favorite wine at the time. The first thing he said when he walked in was: "You have a cat." My place was spotless, but Stevie was right, I did have a cat. I thought I had cleaned the place to perfection.

I had always found Stevie to be so handsome. There he was with a beautiful Afro, designer sunglasses, a meticulously trimmed mustache, wide-collar beautiful bronze and beige long- sleeved silk shirt, tight-fitting tan pants. I insisted he remove his shoes, and I gave him a hand with them. He was a really funny guy who loved to laugh and smiled with genuine ease. We talked about music and drank that Blue Nun; we listened to music and drank more Blue Nun. Then he kissed me, and every fiber of my body responded to that kiss, and beautifully and powerfully, we made love. Just before the sun rose, his brother, Calvin, came to pick him up.

Stevie and I continued to connect, over the years. It wasn't a traditional relationship. I think I wanted more than I was willing to admit. We kept coming together and drifting apart. I was very young and insecure. Also, I was just getting started in the business, just learning how to navigate fame, and Stevie was a bona fide superstar.

Loving Stevie was one of the best experiences of my young life: meeting Stevie, writing songs with Stevie, making love with Stevie. I was sure that I was in love with him, but there were too many girls after him. I was just too naïve to battle for the man I really loved. At his studio, the women would parade in, and of course he always knew they were there. I refused to let Stevie think that I was jealous, so I made myself unavailable. That must have confused him and probably hurt him. I still love Stevie and always will. We remained friends, and even then, I definitely appreciated "a man with a slow hand."

A couple of years later, I had a brief fling with Flip Wilson, the first black entertainer to host a successful weekly variety show. We met on his show, and he invited me to his home in Malibu. I stayed there several nights. We went to the television studio from there in his blue Rolls Royce that he had nicknamed "Killer" (it was even on the license plate). He had the greatest house: a carpeted, heated floor and wall-mounted TV in the bathroom, with sounds of the ocean coming right into the house. His children knew me, and I really wanted him to like me. But when I went on the road and called him, he wouldn't answer. Years later, after his son died in a motorcycle accident, he went through some hard times that included financial issues and substance abuse. Then instead of us opening for him, he ended up as our opening act for a few shows. Later, he started calling me again, but I knew the timing was off. He had other things to deal with.

In 1974, along with James Brown, Bill Withers, Sister Sledge, Al Green, Hugh Masekela, The Spinners, Big Black, the three of us (Bonnie, Ruth, and I) went to Africa as part of the entertainment portion of the Muhammad Ali versus George Foreman fight in Zaire. "The Rumble in the Jungle," the media called it. I was so unprepared for such an extravaganza that I didn't even have a camera with me! Music publicist Gary Stromberg was with us and had a Polaroid camera. He amazed the Africans, taking their pictures and immediately showing them their own image. They wanted anything American, so we traded t-shirts and baseball caps for ivory and malachite. Unfortunately, none of that made it back to the States. I asked our road manager to take care of it, and he turned it over to some locals and that was the end of that. Well, maybe they needed it more than I did.

I sat by the banks of the Congo River and watched the sunset. It was a beautiful river, and one of the most memorable evenings of my life. I also visited a village where the houses, or huts, had no doors—just a piece of fabric over the entrance. There was electricity so they had an extension cord leading from a hut to the front yard where a group of people, old and young, were sitting smoking cannabis and watching TV. I thought this was absolutely fantastic! I loved it and joined them in the celebration. One of the local people taught us to say in French: "Ladies and gentlemen, children too, these brown babies gonna boogie for you." We loved it and started using it in our performances. It even became sort of a catch phrase for us.

The people of Africa loved Muhammad Ali. I loved Muhammad Ali. I loved that he refused to go to the war in Vietnam. He said, "No Vietnamese ever called me 'nigger.'" I don't particularly like the boxing aspect and wouldn't watch it before he came on the scene, but meeting him changed my perspective. He was such a showman and so handsome. Ali asked us to come watch him train every day before the event. He sent his people each day to pick up my sisters and me. We went to the stadium with him to see one of the shows. The crowd went crazy when he walked in, and it was amazing to be there with him. Later, his brother, Rahman, went to Sausalito to my parents' house. I heard that the visit was about me, but alas, Muhammad and

FAIRYTALE

I never did get together.

I had first met him when he came to give a speech at McClymonds High that Fritz had helped organize. I even have a picture somewhere of him holding Jada. Later, he joined us when we were co-hosting the *Mike Douglas Show*. It was so wonderful how our paths continued to cross.

Despite all of the fun we were having, I continued to focus on my songwriting. When I wrote "Fairytale," I wasn't trying to do something clever to break into the country market. I wrote it because that's the way I felt. The lyrics and the melody came to me and I wrote them down. I told the musicians what I wanted them to play. They didn't want to do it that way at first, because it definitely had a "country song" vibe and that was not their jam.

To me, country music is a lot like the music we sang in church with strong melodies and harmonies, and real, relatable stories. I always thought the music, the hymns we sang in church, had a country feel. Also, I used to hear a lot of country music in Arkansas when I lived there in the fifth, seventh, and tenth grades with Grandma. For some reason, I really connected with it and never worried about the fact that it was a different genre. It was just good music.

I only remember listening to one Arkansas radio station and all they played was country music: Hank Williams' "Your Cheatin' Heart," Tex Ritter's "Do Not Forsake Me Oh My Darlin'" and Willie Nelson's "Funny How Time Slips Away." The only time I heard black artists was when I snuck out to the local juke joints and pressed my ear to the door. Grandma forbade me from going inside, but I couldn't imagine why it was so bad. How could it be? I heard songs like Albert King's "I'm a Lonely Man," Chuck Berry's "Maybellene," B.B. King's "Every Day I Have the Blues," Little Richard's "Tutti Frutti," and Fats Domino's "Blueberry Hill."

To me, it was all just good music. With country, the short story format really resonated with me. When I wrote "Shaky Flat Blues," I thought about those songs. "Shaky" is about the difference between living in the country and living in the city, the smells, the sounds. It came out of our experience, Bonnie's and mine, and "Fairytale" was the same way. It was about our personal experience, about accepting the end of a relationship and moving on. The song "Fairytale" was introduced on the May 1974 release of *That's A Plenty* and was written by Bonnie and me. That song became the second of the three Top 40 hits scored by The Pointer Sisters in our original embodiment as a quartet. I sang lead on all three of the hits from that album, and we recorded at Quadraphonic Studios in Nashville. "Fairytale" was obviously a stylistic departure for us, and I knew we were taking a chance.

The album had an iconic cover design of four silhouettes, each bending a knee and pointing a finger. On the back was a photo by photographer Herb Greene that showed the four of us sitting around a table in our signature 1940s' fashions. I am sitting on a Louis Vuitton trunk, holding a handkerchief, Ruth is standing in the middle, Bonnie has a cigarette lighter, and June has a hand in her coat pocket. The track list included "Banging on the Pipes"/"Steam Heat" (medley), "Salt Peanuts," "Grinning in Your Face," "Shaky Flat Blues" (with the four of us receiving writer credit), "That's a Plenty"/"Surfeit, USA" (medley), "Little Pony," "Fairytale" (written by Bonnie and me), "Black Coffee," and "Love in Them There Hills."

We had an amazing group of musicians including Herbie Hancock on piano and Bonnie Raitt on slide guitar. We recorded with David Briggs (piano), Norbert Putnam (bass), Weldon Myrick (pedal steel guitar), Ken Buttrey (drums), Robert Thompson (acoustic guitar), and Norman Spicher (fiddle).

"Fairytale" was not chosen as an advance single as I would have liked. They wanted to stick close to what our audiences had come to expect, so in March 1974, they released "Steam Heat." That was a show tune from the Broadway musical *The Pajama Game*. (It did not become a hit for us until we released our concert album *The Pointer Sisters Live at the Opera House* later the same year. Then it became a signature song for us, and we even performed a medley of "Bubbling Under" and "Steam Heat" on *The Carol Burnett Show*.) The next song released from the *That's a Plenty* album was called "Love in Them There Hills." That, too, failed to attract interest at Pop- or R&B-formatted stations.

I was getting concerned that all of the traction we'd enjoyed in live shows was not translating to the radio format. For some reason, we weren't catching on like I thought we would. Finally, in a brilliant move by David, "Fairytale" was pitched to Country & Western–formatted radio stations. Our record label, Blue Thumb, did not even have a C&W division, but they figured a way around that. ABC Dot Records, another division of the parent company, Famous Music

Group, agreed to release the track to the C&W market.

The song was doing well on country stations and then charted in pop and adult contemporary. However, we knew country was where it fit the best so in support of that single, we began a series of promotional appearances in and around Nashville. We had to reach those fans on their own turf. The issue was that many country listeners did not realize that the women singing the song were African American until we started our local promotional tour. On August 16, 1974, we performed at the Fairgrounds Speedway. Then on October 25, 1974, we had one of the most memorable experiences of our career. We were "special guests" at the Grand Ole Opry in Nashville where we performed "Fairytale." That was the first time, perhaps the last time, an African American vocal group performed there. June, unfortunately, was not able to be a part of that experience because of her health issues.

I was really nervous for that performance because our song had started something of a backlash around Nashville. When we arrived at the Grand Ole Opry, there were protestors carrying signs that said, "Keep Country, Country." It was a jarring sight for us. We had fought during the tumultuous Civil Rights era, which was still fresh in our minds. To see people protesting us because of our race was unsettling. As we took the stage a man screamed, "Hot damn, them girls is black!"

Fortunately, we won the music lovers over with our live performance. I could feel the energy in the room. The audience was obviously taking a "wait and see" attitude. They expected us to earn their respect, and that's what we did. After we performed the song, the same man screamed again, "Sing it again, honey!" And we did. We sang it three more times that night.

During an after-party that included Roy Clark and Dolly Parton, we were mistakenly taken through the back door. The thinking was that we were there as employees to work in the kitchen. We just laughed it off because we were excited to be there. Other than that incident, they really treated us nice. They could see that we were genuine and sincere.

David had some experience working in Nashville and was able to get the song to none other than Elvis Presley. He later recorded and released it on his album *Today* in 1975 and even performed the song at his final show in 1977. We were nominated for two Grammy awards and received our first Grammy in the Country & Western Vocal Performance, Duo, or Group category for "Fairytale." I wrote another country song with Vincent Wayne called "Live Your Life Before You Die." That one was not as well received by the fans, but we did get another Grammy nomination for Best Country Group Performance. We didn't win, but it was great to be recognized in that genre. Today, that song has a place in the African American Museum of History and Culture in Washington, DC, along with a photo of us receiving our award. Now, that's quite an honor!

Our star was definitely on the rise, but it was not all fun and games. It involved a lot of hard work and perseverance. In July of 1974, we had one of the most hectic schedules of any artists that summer. However, we were determined to take advantage of the momentum we were experiencing so we made it a priority to give our best at every performance. Here's a sample of what that time was like for us.

On July 25-28, we headlined at the Universal Studios Amphitheater in Los Angeles. The same week we taped an appearance on a Nancy Wilson TV special to be shown in August. Next, we flew cross-country to appear at Atlantic City's Club Harlem on August 5-11. Then it was back to L.A. to tape a special, "Live at the Palladium," to air on NBC on September 6. While we were there, we taped an appearance on *The Carol Burnett Show*, as well as a special for the Public Broadcasting Service (PBS) and appeared in a promotional film. Following that, we went to Philadelphia to tape a week's worth of co-hosting on *The Mike Douglas Show* for an early September airing. Still moving fast, we had a series of concerts lined up for New Jersey, plus an appearance at the Central Park Schaefer Music Festival on August 30, not to mention the American Song Festival in Saratoga Springs, Florida the next night.

Being co-hosts on the *Mike Douglas Show* was great fun for us and any time we were on TV it helped raise our public profile. As co-hosts, we were able to make guest requests. We ended up with Muhammad Ali, Angela Davis, our cousin Paul Silas (who was then with the Boston Celtics), and even our parents. It was a treat beyond compare to be able to sing with our parents on the show. We did one of mom's favorite songs, "The Uncloudy Day." Mother and Dad loved this song and sang it with conviction. After all, they knew all about "storm clouds" and "cloudy days" from their days in Arkansas all the way to Oakland, California. Now, after a mere four years in show business and a frenzied touring pace, there was a ray of sunlight. The only dark spot was that June was under the weather and not able to join us. We were a trio once again.

Oh, they tell me of a home far beyond the skies Oh, they tell me of a home far away

Oh, they tell me of a home where no storm clouds rise Oh, they tell me of an uncloudy day.

Originally written by J.K. Alwood in 1885, "The Uncloudy Day" was covered by Willie Nelson on his 1976 *Troublemaker* album. Mother and Dad sang this song with reverent sincerity during the *Mike Douglas Show*. It was an unforgettable experience.

To finish up that year, we had an appearance on *Soul Train* and a headline engagement at the Dallas Fairmont Hotel. Then we were off on a European concert tour September 20 to October 12 and a swing through Japan November 15 through 26.

That's a Plenty went gold that August, and then we released the double live album, *The Pointer Sisters Live at the Opera House*. We toured the U.S. four times, and I can tell you it was beyond grueling. No matter how excited we were to be doing the work, my body was tired, I was mentally exhausted, tired of being sick and tired. Poor June collapsed from the strain. She was unusually thin, and she seemed unable to concentrate. We were worried about her and she was checked into Mt. Zion Hospital in San Francisco. They found out that because of a kidney issue, she was losing weight rapidly and was down to 90 pounds.

Just as we were getting a taste of fame, we were feeling the negative effects as well. In November 1975, magazines and newspapers around the country published articles with headlines like: "June Pointer is Pooped" and "One Pointer Sister Plans to Leave Act," and "Pointer Sister Retires" and "June Plans to Quit Pointer Sisters Act." All the reports were similar. They claimed that at age 22, June was giving up performing live and retiring from the stage due to extreme physical and mental exhaustion. That wasn't true, of course. We were only focused on getting June better. No other decisions had been made, but the truth does not always make for a compelling headline.

Even with the success of *That's A-Plenty*, we continued working with other artists as well. To me, it was smart businesswise to remain flexible and work on anything that appealed to us, regardless of whether we were singing lead or headlining a show. We contributed background vocals to the song "Daylight" which was a top-five R&B hit for Bobby Womack. We had a fun appearance on the PBS children's show *Sesame Street* where we sang the "Pinball Court" song. I brought my daughter Jada, and Ruth brought Faun and Malik to the session. They all ended up singing on that song which made it even more special to us.

We continued to appear regularly on *The Carol Burnett Show*. We sang "Salt Peanuts" and a Nat King Cole song called "Save the Bones for Henry Jones" which we had learned from our adopted brother, Mudavanha. We weren't just there to sing, either. Once we were in a comedy sketch with Carol called "Cinderella Gets It On." We were Cinderella's wicked stepsisters.

We were such a hit on the show that Carol took us on the road with her as the opening act. At first, we were concerned because we were used to wearing different outfits for each performance to give the audience something new. However, that's not the way it worked on Carol's show. She only had two wardrobe changes and that was it. It wasn't a fashion show. It was comedy.

With every new experience, and every new artist we worked with, we learned something about the business of entertainment. I was enjoying our newfound popularity, but I also kept an eye on our longevity. I wanted to make sure we did a great job every time. It was important that we didn't get a reputation as being difficult or late or unprofessional. I was determined to ensure that we held ourselves to a high standard no matter what was going on around us. We needed to continue growing by making smart business decisions.

After all, I was sure it was only a matter of time before June would be back in the fold.

Chapter 9

A BACKWARD LIFE

AS OUR POPULARITY CONTINUED TO BUILD, I REALIZED THAT A lot of it was a result of being in the right place and the right time and having our own unique look and sound. Our style came from the old days of radio-land, when there was a thing called female vocal harmony that was all the rage through the '30s and '40s, as evidenced by the many "sister" groups: The Andrews Sisters, Boswell Sisters, Clark Sisters, de Castro Sisters, and on and on. It was definitely a trend at that time and one we thought was due for a return.

With nostalgia gaining in popularity, especially among the younger generation who seemed to get a kick out of dressing like their parents and grandparents, our style was coming into vogue and our outfits only helped to fuel that interest. We dressed that way initially because we wanted to stand out and those were the "fancy" clothes that our relatives had stowed away in trunks and the backs of closets. That meant they were free, which was about all we could afford at the time. Fortunately, our fashion choices worked perfectly with our image and sound.

The more positive responses we got, the more we played up our fashions. We started including fake flowers, boas, large "church hats," and more of those beautifully tailored vintage dresses. When audiences saw these tall, dark beauties in coordinating fashions, it only added to our uniqueness and made people take notice.

Bonnie liked to say, "We went from old to young: old clothes, old music to new clothes and new music. It was like we lived our lives backward, from traditional music and clothes to modern music and clothes. We started out old, like little old ladies, singing old music and became young." She cracked up laughing, "That's funny as hell to me. This dress thing has been wrongly interpreted by some. Some people think we're trying to create nostalgia or re-creation of past times, but it was not that at all. We dressed that way years ago, because we couldn't afford to dress better. We haunted thrift shops, and we sort of naturally developed a taste for '40s clothing. Now that we're not dependent on secondhand clothing anymore, there doesn't seem to be any reason to change our style. So, we had the same stuff made by a designer now. Everything sure fits better."

Our musical taste was also a result of us coming together. Bonnie said, "We sang rock for so long, yet when we'd start to write it didn't come out like that. We wrote 'Jada' for Anita's daughter and it sounds much closer to Lambert, Hendricks, and Ross than any other composer. We were into using our voices as instruments and at one point in the show fooled audiences by 'playing' toy trumpets and saxophones. No, that was us singing; those toys don't make any noise at all."

It's true that we took a lot of chances with our songs. We would mix in different things to make it interesting and see how the audience responded. Our look and our sound were already unique so we thought it would work for us, and it usually did. In a song called "That's How I Feel" we didn't even sing words, almost like the scatting of the older songs. We would basically have conversations in a song without any discernable words. It also helped to play on our sisterhood, like we had a language all our own.

Bonnie said, "It's all gibberish, but it makes sense to us. Sometimes we go around the house singing to each other in scat instead of talking, so that song just came naturally. We didn't plan what we were going to say, and it came out differently each time, sort of spontaneous improvisation. After a 45-minute show, we were ready to do it again in minutes. Singing like ours comes naturally to all of us and as for the power of our voices, well, you have to remember, Mom and Dad were both preachers and we're preachers' daughters. We got to be heard."

By 1974, with our second album *That's A Plenty* doing well, we finally made a little money. That year, as a group we grossed just over a million dollars. With that money, we moved Dad, 73, Mom, 50, Grandma Roxie, 83, and Ruth's daughter Faun and son Malik, and my daughter Jada into a fine, five-bedroom house in Sausalito overlooking the San Francisco Bay.

We weren't rich by any means because out of that income we had to support a band, road manager, sound and lighting engineers, wardrobe person, travel and hotel costs, a Sausalito mortgage, as well as expenses for the new family house, but we knew that the first thing we would do was take care of the family. That's what we were always all about. When it came right down to it, nothing else mattered.

Just because 1974 had been our first good year financially didn't mean we could relax. We started off 1975 by playing a show at the Venetian Room of the Dallas Fairmont Hotel from January 25 through 31. The show was sold out every night and with June still out of commission, we were more determined than ever to deliver a great performance. We didn't want a repeat of that horrible time in Vegas.

Our '40s musical style was on full display as we opened the show with songs like our hits "Salt Peanuts," "Sunny Side of the Street," and "Swaying with Sammy Kaye." We liked starting the show with up-tempo songs that got the crowd going. Those songs were also wonderful vehicles for our harmonies, which of course were second nature for us. Just to throw in something outlandish, we wore hats made of plastic fruit a la Carmen Miranda as we sang "Chattanooga Choo-Choo" and the audience loved it.

We enjoyed performing songs by some of the great artists of that era. A lot of people have the nerve to ask us if we wrote some of the Ellington tunes because they seemed so much a part of us. So, sometimes we had to educate people musically as well as entertain them. We turned people on to a lot of things that have made music history like "Steam Heat" and the "Duke Ellington Medley," and of course Dizzy Gillespie's "Salt Peanuts."

One thing we did differently that time was that we didn't wear our retro fashions. Instead we wore fancy blue metallic dresses that Carol Burnett had given us after an appearance on her show. As with many of her outfits, they were designed by Bob Mackie and they had beautiful feathers along one arm. To complete the look, we had added eye-catching top hats. We included more choreography than usual, and as expected, the crowd loved it. It was yet another experiment with our act, trying out new things to gauge the audience's response.

Maybe it was the sight of us in glittery, bespoke outfits while singing classic songs like "Steam Heat" that added to our uniqueness as a group of African American sisters singing, harmonizing, and now dancing in perfect uniformity. Our performance was tight, and the reception was more than we could have expected. We were amazed by the enthusiastic response. Everything had come together perfectly, all the moving parts working in unison to create a phenomenal show.

It had been just over a year since we had started our act, and while we did make some good money, we had also accumulated plenty of debt. We owed David Rubinson over $100,000, which included financial support for us and our family for six months before we even had our first public appearance.

"I don't think of the money advanced to them as a loan," David said, "it's venture capital. I have invested, on behalf of my corporation, in a business in which I believe and which I think will make a profit; very likely, substantial profits. It was only after the Opera House that The Pointer Sisters began operating at a profit."

It would take us until about September of 1975 to get out of that initial debt burden. David called it an advance, but all advances are basically interest-free loans because they have to be paid back. Regardless, we were grateful for the opportunities and determined to take full advantage of them. Having my sisters with me helped us to distribute the load when dealing with the money, fame, and negative aspects of the business. I definitely assumed a more business-like approach, trying to make sure that no matter how crazy things became, we still came across as professionals who did not let down their audiences.

My sisters were also concerned with the act, but with money coming in, their attention often shifted to focusing on their own families and enjoying the fruits of our labor. I understood that and championed us to at least control the costs of our shows. We continued to wear the older costumes occasionally, and if we did splurge on new outfits, the goal was not to exceed $150 even for a custom-made gown.

We were having fun, but not what I'd call getting wild. We drank, smoked cigarettes, and occasionally had a little pot. Our success was something we had worked hard for, and we wanted to enjoy it. However, our mother thought we were working too much. In an interview way back in 1975, she said to the *Marin Independent Journal*, "They are being pushed too hard; they get tired. Sometimes they do not get enough sleep because of two shows at night and interviews during the day." She was concerned about us as any mother would be, especially about her youngest.

June had been home in Sausalito since October of 1974 recuperating from the mental, physical, and emotional strain of performing. "I'm getting all the rest I can now; I am saving it up. When we were on tour, we go to theaters for one or two shows every night," she had said. Then she laughed about the time Sammy Davis Jr. called Mother to make arrangements to escort The Pointer Sisters to Liza Minelli's wedding reception. Mother said to him, "Are you really Sammy Davis Jr.? Don't lie now, remember my heart." Of course it was Sammy and we ended up spending the night at his house. It was an amazing experience!

At twenty-two, June understood that being an entertainer was hard work. After we'd been on the road for three weeks straight, she said, "We're on the road more than airline stewardesses. But the fun part was doing shows like *Carol Burnett* and the *Cher Show*. Our party was on stage. Getting all dressed up and then seeing the results was exciting. Getting paid for it was kind of fun, too!"

June remained out of commission for six months. Her timing was good for us because we were excited about the release of our third album, *Steppin'* in 1975. With that album, we were experimenting with changing things up. Not too much, but enough to show that we were ready for new artistic challenges. Even the cover heralded a new era with the image of black and purple sling-back high-heel Converse-style shoes. Then the back picture was the underside of the shoes, showing metals taps on the heel and toe. It was the mid-70s and disco was just picking up steam. I knew that if we wanted longevity, we needed to be versatile with our image and our sound.

I felt like that album was a true expression of who we were at the time and what we stood for. Bonnie and I wrote the first single "How Long (Betcha' Got a Chick on the Side)," and I sang lead. It definitely had a soul and R&B vibe, but there was no mistaking the hint of disco sprinkled in. That combination must have worked because that single went to number 20 on the *US Billboard Hot 100* and spent two weeks at the number 1 spot on the *Hot Soul Singles* chart. (The song was later sampled by Salt-N-Pepa and recorded by Queen Latifah.) We did a fun medley tribute to Duke Ellington with "I Ain't Got Nothing but the Blues." The second single released was an epic, eight-minute-long gospel-tinged song called "Going Down Slowly" written by Allen Toussaint which went to number 61 on the *Billboard Hot 100* and num-

A BACKWARD LIFE

ber 16 on the R&B chart. The ditty "Save the Bones for Henry Jones" was written by Danny Barker and Michael Goldson and popularized in the 50s by Nat King Cole and Johnny Mercer.

June did a lovely lyrical rendering of "Wanting Things" by Burt Bacharach, and Bonnie and I wrote lyrics to add to Isaac Hayes' instrumental "Ellie's Love Theme" from *Shaft*, and we named it "Easy Days." (That song was later turned into "The Hood Gone Love It" by Kendrick Lamar, and he won the Pulitzer Prize in 2018 for his work in hip-hop.) Once again, Herbie Hancock contributed by playing clavinet on the Latin-flavored version of Taj Mahal's "Chainey Do." I sang lead on the Stevie Wonder song "Sleeping Alone" while he played electric piano, which was an inside nod to our shared past. Overall, the album went to number 22 on the *US Billboard 200* and number 3 on the *US Billboard Top R&B/Hip-Hop Albums*.

That was a particularly fun time for us, not because the album was doing so well, but because we were so excited to have the family together in the new house where they didn't have to worry about anything. For the last two years, we had been leasing a beautiful five-bedroom home at 26 Cloudview Road in Sausalito, overlooking the harbor, for Mom and Dad, Grandma Roxie, Faun, Malik, and Jada. Now the new house was being built for them in Marin County, Novato. Our parents had lost their church and taken various jobs to earn an income. It felt really good that our success was paying off for them as well. At the time, June said, "We saw them lose their church, their home, and their daughters. They had to move into an icky house in the deep slums. To be able to bring them out of that...that was a good feeling." During that time, Mother wrote a few letters to Fritz that perfectly documented what was going on in their lives.

On January 30, 1976, Mother wrote:

Hi Fritz,

It was so good hearing from you. We are all fine and happy. Packing like mad. Anita finally got all of the papers in and we hope to move next weekend. We talked with Shegun and Nandi [Fritz and Barbara's children] last week and they will be over today. June will leave Sunday a.m. to meet the girls in Fort Lauderdale, Florida. She is really excited about the trip. She's been hanging out at the Record Plant, a recording studio here in Sausalito – which I thought was good. Some group called her and asked her to come down and jam with them, so she went. Good. Good. Don't you think so?

FAIRYTALE

The children here are fine. Faun's birthday is tomorrow, January 31st. She will be eleven. Sister Tires had a heart attack and she is in the hospital, doing better, but complete bed rest. Uncle Jack and Aunt Della are doing just fine, working and really getting things together. I don't know about Uncle Leon. Things are kind of hard for him at his age.

Mother (Grandma Roxie) is doing fine – she sure misses you and we all do, Fritz. I didn't realize how attached I had gotten to you. Boy I miss you so bad. But I know it isn't for a lifetime; so, do your best son, we are praying for you. Prayer changes things. Pastor Small said he will write you before long.

Daddy is fine. The usual Dad sleep...sleep and more sleep. Oh well, you can't win them all. Fritz, I will mail your box off next week; and also send you some money. Baby, keep sweet and ask God to give you true love...love...real love casts out fear: for fear is torment.

The girls are still working on a new contract, so I am praying that the Lord will work everything out for their good. I didn't yet but as soon as I talk to them again, I will remind them to remember you through these trying times. I do hope that you get a job real soon.

God bless you my son and remember: God is Love and Love is God.
Be Sweet,
Mother

Our brother Fritz had acted as our road manager for about six months because we were trying to help him out with employment, but our management fired him. The problem was that he didn't warn us and the crew about holes in the Madison Square Garden stage. One of his main responsibilities was staking out upcoming venues and preparing the entire crew with all the necessary information to get ready for the show. His next offense was that he refused a request to go for burgers during the taping of an episode of *The Carol Burnett Show* so he could finish reading his *New York Times*. It worked out for the best because he had his eye on an academic career. He soon moved to Madison, Wisconsin to pursue a post-graduate degree in African Literature at the university and landed a job as an Adult Basketball League referee.

On February 3, 1976, Mother wrote:

Hi Fritz,

We are fine. The kids were over this weekend. They're fine. I do hope that things are working out for you. We didn't get moved yet, but everything is packed...hardly anything to eat out of. Dear, enclosed find a little eating money

from Dad and me. We love you and...Oh boy do I miss you.
    Your Mom

Before leaving for Madison, Fritz had lived with Mom and Dad and the rest in Sausalito. He had been a reliable chauffer shuttling Mother back and forth to San Francisco to visit June in the hospital and helping to care for her when Mother insisted and said to the doctors, "I'm taking my baby home." That was some two years ago; now, they were moving into a new house bought for them by The Pointer Sisters. We put $40,000 down, $10,000 from each of us. This time we were buying, not renting, and it was in one of the wealthiest counties in the U.S. The entire family was excited.

February 14, 1976:

Hi Fritz,

We finally moved. Everybody is tired, tired. I received your beautiful letter; we all enjoyed reading it. Did you hear that we had snow in Sausalito? A day before we moved it snowed real, real hard.

The kids made a snowman. Ruthie was here to help us move. She looks real good. Anita is home, too, and looking good. We are very happy in our new home: neighbors are just beautiful, so nice to us. All white so far. Grandma isn't too good: she wandered away from the house yesterday. Dad and I were out.

She broke her right wrist and it's very painful. She's real feeble. The kids are fine; I've tried to call Barbara [Fritz's former wife] several times and didn't get her yet. I'll keep trying. We are without a phone until Monday, but it will be installed before you get our letter. San Francisco State called you about a job.

Your friend, Simon, also called – also, Humboldt University. But I think that you made the wiser decision. I paid two months on your Sears revolving account, Jan. & Feb., so that is paid up until March. What do you pay on your other Sears bill? How much a month? Well dear, just to let you know that we are now in Novato, #1 David Court, 94947.

Love You,

Mother

Once they moved into the house, we had a few more things to work out. We told Mother she would need to give up her janitorial job in Oakland, along with her pension, and be provided for by The Pointer Sisters. We followed our family's philosophy: "If I'm blessed, you're blessed."

Mother sounded stronger and more confident with each letter.

March 12, 1976

Hi Mr. Pointer,

How is Madison and the world treating you? We are fine as can be and enjoying this beautiful little town. We love Novato. Oh, everything is so nice: the people are so friendly, and it is home. Thank God for all of you children. God has been so good to us.

Fritz, I can't forget to thank Him for His love to us and for giving us such wonderful children. I am proud of all of you. I don't forget to thank my God daily for smiling on me and blessing me with a family who love each other. It's a wonderful and good feeling.

Fritz, it was so good to talk with you today. I miss you still so very much. Listen boy, you spoiled me. And, every time I see an orange Volvo, I look to see if it's you. Malik is doing okay now; he dropped 50lbs of weights on his right baby finger: messed up a nerve and had to have seven stitches; but he's doing better now. We've all had terrible colds; Grandma is doing very well; mine very bad, but she is close to us, and the kids can ride their bikes to see her; so they go often. I do hope you have a lovely trip to Chicago.

During this time, we were working in Ft. Lauderdale. June had agreed to fly down and join us. She was in good spirits and seemed well rested. It amazed me how we all got along so well. We would yell and get in fights occasionally, but once we got things off our chest, we went back to being sisters. It just worked out for us like that.

On April 24, 1976, we were back in the Bay Area, joined by the hot new reggae sounds of the East Bay Shakers to open the month of May under the stars at the Concord Pavilion. This was different from our most recent dates in San Francisco six months earlier when we did a four-night run at Bimbo's club to standing-room only and slightly hysterical audience. This May 1, 1976 appearance at the Pavilion was themed "Picnic Under the Stars with The Pointer Sisters." It was designed to appeal to their large and very widespread Bay Area following by providing the beautifully open, fresh-air atmosphere that was the new Concord Pavilion. It was an amazing show, but not everything was perfect in the world of show business.

On September 15, 1976, Mother wrote to Fritz with an early hint at the issues developing with our management:

Hi Hon,

Things are looking better; for a while I didn't know even about myself. So sorry it took me so long, but better late than never...huh! The children are all fine and back in school. Dad isn't too well...has a terrible cold. Mother is hanging in there. The girls are mad, but fine: still having their problems with David Rubinson. I hope things are better for you.

I love you, Fritz, and I wish you success and happiness. I'll write again soon. Just wanted to get this in the mail. So, as soon as the Lord blessed me, I included my son.

Love Always,

Mother

On October 26, 1976, the focus was June's fragile health and all of our personal business:

Hi Fritz,

Received your letter today: So very glad to hear from you. Things are looking up: didn't look too good for a while but thank God He still answered prayers. June has been very, very sick...at death's door! I was in Los Angeles for about two weeks. She was very sick. This time it wasn't mental, it was infected ovaries. Doctors thought that they would have to operate, but we prayed, and I went down and I stayed, and I stayed by her bedside, morning, noon and night for ten nights. She missed the show here in Frisco at the Fairmont: the other girls carried on; they did a good job. Things still aren't the best for them either – David is still messing with their money.

Fritz, Dr. Young is really on our case about Shegun's dental bill. I gave him $50.00 last week. Barbara said Dr. Young also talked to her about the bill. Shegun's teeth are looking good; he's still treating them. I am having some work done on my teeth, $600.00 also. But I am going to do the best I can about your dental bill for Shegun. Oh, so we're getting serious about Liz. All right! I want the best for you. I love you very much and whoever you love, I love; and if she can make you happy. Okay!

Ruth is staying at Bonnie and June's: here is their address and phone number (Hollywood, CA). Most times they are all at their boyfriends' addresses. June's boyfriend is a huckster. Be careful. His phone number is XXXXXX. You can, most of the time, get June there. Call her collect sometimes, after five. They are doing the Carol Burnett Show, *now. Bonnie is going with a young man named Jeffrey Bowen. His phone number is XXXXXXX. Anita is with a guy named Sunny Burke. His phone number is XXXXXXX. all Los Angeles* numbers. *Ruth is having trouble with her man, so she's at June's and Bonnie's place.*

I talked with Shegun and Nandi Sunday night. They will be over this week-end. Daddy is doing fine: he's helping me a lot more since I had to go away: he sees now what I was doing. Sister Lee stayed here and helped him while I was away. Mother is doing alright.

Oh, I guess you saw where Paul (Silas) was sold to Denver: sold or traded: didn't see any money or prices. He wanted three million, I heard. Oh well, to each his own. Tell Liz it sure will be nice when we can get the chance to meet her. Yes, Shegun likes the family very much...he and Nandi speak often about them. Faun, Malik and Jada are fine.

We Love You Dear,
Mother

As evidenced by the letters, she was the family barometer, thinking of everybody. Nobody was excluded. She knew how her children were doing, and her children's children, her nephews and nieces. She knew, or wanted to know, the status of everyone. She kept up with all of us girls from our ever-changing romantic lives to our globe-trotting career.

After the hit show in Concord, we were off to Las Vegas and then on a worldwide tour that included both the Far East (Manila, Singapore, Bangkok, Hong Kong, and Japan) and Europe (Antwerp, Belgium, the Netherlands, London, and Paris). While in Europe we filmed a live satellite cable show that even reached 1.5 million homes in the United States. We also had to return to Los Angeles to tape television variety shows with Andy Williams and Mac Davis and work on our next album for ABC Records. We also found out that we might be in a movie.

Aida was a producer for Don Cornelius' *Soul Train*. She had a friend, Gary Stromberg, who had been our press rep since the beginning. He was producing a new film called *Car Wash*. This was in 1976 and the cast would include Richard Pryor and be directed by Michael Schultz. One day, when we were visiting Aida, Gary came by and I had heard about the film. So, we just asked him, "Why don't you put us in the movie?" Just like that...and he did! The Pointer Sisters appeared as The Wilson Sisters: four glamorous singers who accompanied the smooth-talking preacher "Daddy Rich" played by Richard Pryor.

A BACKWARD LIFE

That's how it happens sometimes, you know, in the right place and being ready. We were in the right place, and we were beyond ready! Filming was so much fun. Oh my God, working with Richard Pryor. He was so excited. He had the cast laughing all the time. We went to his house and hung out with him. Making that movie was one of the best experiences of my career: acting, singing, and doing that movie with Michael Schultz, the director. Most of the cast were young and eager, just like us. Along with Richard there was Bill Duke, George Carlin, Antonio Fargas, Garrett Morris, and Danny DeVito. It was an eclectic cast of young, edgy Hollywood actors and we were all just excited to be there. We had such a good time partying one night that we didn't even go to sleep. Then we got a call the next morning that they needed to film some close-ups. Luckily, we were young back then, because after a hard night, we had to get not just camera ready, but close-up ready!

I had no idea if the movie was going to be successful or not. There were a lot of movies of that genre of blaxploitation films, so it was definitely on trend with what was going on in movies with titles like *Foxy Brown* and *Cooley High*. I wasn't thinking about whether it would be a big hit. I just thought it was a good career move for us, and I found out quickly that exposure was always good for our business.

Of course, the movie was a big hit and has gained a large following even though it was filmed back in 1976. We were only in the entire movie for about seven minutes, mainly stepping out of a gold stretch limo with Richard when he drove up to the carwash to share the gospel. We were his entourage.

Just a few years ago, I was in Los Angeles actually getting my car washed, and who did I run into but my *Car Wash* co-star Bill Duke! We both had a good laugh about that coincidence and caught up on old times. Bill wrote a little poem for me when I told him I was writing a book.

The Pointer Sisters were a joy to work with on Car Wash,
The Pointer Sisters and Richard Pryor
Tortured me in that film Car Wash
But when beautiful, talented women
Torture you
It feels good.

The movie worked well into our overall career because we were really getting attention. We were constantly in demand for more TV show appearances, we had a new record, and we were always touring because live shows were where we always shined. The song from *Car Wash*, "You Gotta Believe," made the R&B top 20 in early 1977, and we had originally hoped to perform the title song, "Car Wash." That honor went to the group Rose Royce; although, during their recording session, we were told they were asked to sing it like The Pointer Sisters!

Following *Car Wash*, we had to head back into the studio to record our fifth album called *Having a Party* which came out in 1977. This time, we worked with David Rubinson to create a more contemporary R&B and funk album, still using our harmonies, but with less of the retro songs. June only sang on the title song, not any of the other material. That was not the only difficulty we had.

We worked hard on that record and did a lot of writing with the hope that it would reach a new audience. Ultimately there were only seven tracks: "Having a Party" a Sam Cooke song; "Don't It Drive You Crazy"; "I Need a Man," with writing credits that included David, me, Bonnie, and June; "Waiting on You," written with Ruth; "I'll Get by Without You," credited to Bonnie; "Bring Your Sweet Stuff Home to Me," by Stevie Wonder, Bonnie, and me; and finally "Lonely Gal" written by me, Bonnie, and Ruth.

Unfortunately, Blue Thumb records, which had been purchased by ABC-Dunhill in late 1974, was practically non-existent at that point. The album ended up being delayed, which meant it did not come out until a year and a half after our last album, "Steppin'." That was not good for us. I was worried that we were losing the career momentum we had worked so hard to build. *Having a Party* didn't chart any hit singles and was soon forgotten. The only bright note was that "Don't It Drive You Crazy," with Bonnie singing lead, became a cult hit in the UK.

I had been excited for the album initially and sang lead on "I Need a Man" and "Baby Bring Your Sweet Stuff Home to Me"; I also sang lead on "Waiting on You," which was one of the few songs that really meant a lot to me. Once when we were playing The Bottom Line in New York City, we were in the middle of a sound check. Then we left the stage and went to the dressing room. Ruth remained onstage because the band was just jamming, and the rhythm was so great. She came up with some of the lyrics to that song. Then I joined and we finished it together because I was in a relationship where I was always waiting on the man. He'd say he was coming over, but I was always waiting. Sometimes he'd show up and sometimes he wouldn't.

It's often the difficulties in life that provide the best material for writing songs.

Chapter 10

FIRE

I N 1976, MOTHER'S INTUITION SENSED THE TENSION AND MALAISE brewing within our group and wrote to Fritz, on January 31, 1977:

Mr. Fritz H. Pointer

Hi Son,

At this writing I am so very tired but encouraged to press on. Daddy isn't well, but able to be up. Aunt Della is here with me. She had her operation, it was successful, and she is doing better; a long way to go for she really had a serious operation.

The girls are fine: they're singing together. It's not like it should be, but they are trying to make the best of it right now, for they all need the money. They will be on T.V. next Friday night. They're also going to Colorado, out from Denver – Wed. Thurs. & Fri.

Paul (Silas) was over to see us when he was here. He said May 7th is his Anniversary date. He gave me this address and phone # to give to you. Bonnie has her boyfriend as her manager – I guess –and he is making a real fool out of her, they say: $1,400 dress, $500.00 purse and $800.00 shoes. Can you dig this? Anita can't stand him. So, he just bosses Bonnie real good.

June is doing nicely, so far. Well dear, you be sweet. The kids are fine. Faun's birthday is tomorrow, Jan. 31, Malik's Dec. 15, Ruthie March 19, Anita Jan. 23, Aaron April 19, Daddy April 2, June...Guess when? Bonnie is July 11, so now you have them, again.

November 1977 began a series of lasts for The Pointer Sisters in many ways. *Having A Party* would be the last album to feature Bonnie as a member of the group, the last album to feature David Rubinson as our producer, and the last album we recorded for Blue Thumb. The professional relationship seemed to have run its course after the last album produced no major hits nor had strong sales. Bonnie and June were dead-set on leaving David and finding new management. We weren't making the money that all of us felt we should be making. We all agreed on that point. However, I was the one who went to all the business meetings and helped with the banking and the contracts.

I tried to explain that we weren't making the money because of the agreement we had made. So, it wasn't necessarily David's fault. I thought we should renegotiate with him and work out a better arrangement instead of totally changing managers and starting over. That's when Bonnie and June even accused me of being somehow responsible for the lack of funds. We all knew that we were famous, but nearly broke. That was not a good look, because of course people expected us to be doing well and we just weren't.

One of the reasons for our lack of income was that David wanted the best musicians possible for us, which we appreciated. We just didn't realize that paying them meant little money, if any, was left for us. Our club appearances were not big money makers and the band was getting the lion's share of revenue from their work in the studio. At one point, our pianist, Tom Salisbury, quit the band because he said he didn't like the way we were being treated in that whole equation. We were working like crazy, but the financial rewards were nonexistent.

"As far as the parting," Rubinson said, "it wasn't amicable, because I was spoken to very harshly by someone. I was fired by someone who hadn't put in five years and every dime he ever had in the world. I feel bad about it. I'm pleased The Pointer Sisters are doing so well. They're breaking new ground, they're stretching past the normal limits, and they're working with top people, which is where they belong."

The seminal years that David Rubinson provided were truly a training ground for us. His management gave us the professionalism, the confidence, the experiential infrastructure (showing up sober, on-time and prepared, schedules, and touring) and freedom to leave the solid shore of tradition for the tumultuous and competitive waters of uncharted territory for us. We were transitioning our focus from jazz to pop. That may in part explain why we always had an ambiguous relationship with "the black community," particularly in Oakland, California.

Possibly because of our determination to cross musical genres, we were never considered "a black singing group." We weren't part of Motown, we didn't stay in the R&B/Soul genre, and we appealed to all types of audiences. We were unintentionally crossing many barriers and changing perceptions of what to expect from an all-female black singing group. Starting with our retro fashions, we were not the norm and it was hard to label us, which confused the entertainment industry. Remember browsing through record stores back in the day? Performers were actually defined by genre and stocked only in that section. It was a literal manifestation of the tendency to assume musical artists can only appeal to a certain demographic. The thought was that otherwise, how would music buyers know where to find our records?

We had already won awards and had hit records in genres like jazz, blues, R&B, and even country. Despite having a big hit with "Fairytale" and winning a Grammy, country music fans wouldn't have found our album in that section of the store. There was no easy solution, and my concern for our group was whether we were making the best business decisions for our career. I knew the type of songs that worked best for us, and they crossed genres. So, do we only record and perform one type of music or stretch ourselves creatively? I also had to keep in mind that we had been blessed with this amazing career, and we were able to share that with our family. It was now our responsibility to not only keep our career going, but to see just how far we could go.

David Rubinson had provided the foundation, the infrastructure, the armature for us to do that. We had been fortunate to have him in our corner, but now we were at a career crossroads. I was determined, despite June's health and Bonnie leaving, that we were not going to sit back and just sing our previous hits. I had a feeling that we could do more and reach an even wider audience than we already had. However, I also knew that one or two bad business decisions and our career could be quickly derailed.

The impending issue was internal. Bonnie wanted to leave the group and June's health was fragile. We had already proved that we could perform as a trio if necessary, and we did many times. I could accept that as our reality, but if we didn't have June, things would be much more difficult. We had only been working with David for five years, from 1971 to 1976, and to be honest, I don't think Bonnie ever really gave him a chance. It had seemed like a lifetime because so much changed for us during that period, but it was only a few years. With Bonnie leaving and us being between managers, I knew we had to come up with a plan. At the beginning, we were so young, so naïve, and David had been so good to us. Now things were going to be much different.

I was frustrated with my sisters because I was always in the position of playing the mother of the group, and I took it seriously. I worked very hard to only do things that would be in all of our best interests. Also, when it came to singing lead and writing songs, I was doing most of that, but I never tried to stand out and take credit. It was important that we were viewed as a group, not a lead singer with backup. That was not what we were about. I was willing to compromise and do the work for the good of the group, but it didn't seem like everyone had the same idea.

At first Bonnie's departure was a shock for me and difficult to understand. We always had our family squabbles, but in the end, we would come together and work it out. Professionally, we were careful to share in performing duties, alternating lead vocals when it fit our voices and sharing in songwriting and other choices. I always encouraged us to do what was best for the song and had no problem sharing the spotlight. I had been eager to join Bonnie and June on stage and become part of the act, and now it seemed like it was down to Ruth and me.

Bonnie always had an independent streak. We all knew that being together and working together and always compromising could be difficult. I think she wanted to learn more about herself and stretch herself creatively. She wanted to do things on her own, which I certainly understood. I only wish she had left the group in a different way. We were in Chicago to do a show, waiting for Bonnie to arrive. She called and said she was not coming. That was how she left the group. We had to rearrange our vocal parts and our sound-check at the very last minute. Ruthie, June, and I pulled together and did the show, but I didn't like doing that to the audience. I didn't want it to be a gamble as to which sisters would show up at any given concert.

After our return to L.A., June said if Bonnie wasn't coming back, then she was leaving too, and she did! That's when everything that we'd worked so hard for started to unravel right before our eyes. I pleaded with June to come back. This was a crucial time for us because we were trying to find new management and our group was crumbling. The irony was that Bonnie and June were the ones who wanted us to leave David and after we did, they ended up leaving the group. So that meant we were without any management at all.

Sonny Burke, who was a producer on one of our albums, introduced us to a man named Forrest Hamilton because he knew we were looking for new management. Forrest agreed to be our manager and he told us there was a deal brewing with a producer named Steve Wax. From there, we met a man named Richard Perry. Richard is a record producer from Brooklyn, New York who was well-established in the music business having worked with artists like Carly Simon, Barbra Streisand, Diana Ross, Martha Reeves, Leo Sayer, and many others. We met with him and said we were interested in joining his new record label, Planet Record. There was just one problem. We were down two sisters. June said, "It was because of the workload. It was too much work for me at that time. So, I would just say, 'No, I'm not going.'"

Mother sensed deeply the condition of her children: all six of her children, and their children. Bonnie had left the group and June was following her. Daddy was not doing well, and she had to bring in a hospital bed and care for him with the help of Rose Gibson. This, and the struggle to stay afloat financially, was taking a toll on her health.

On February 2, 1978, Mother wrote to Fritz:

Hi Fritz, Liz and Shegun,

How are you today? Oh well, I do feel better: not well, but better. At least I'm home now; the doctor said I just made it, and I will have to stay in for at least three weeks – don't even go outdoors. Anita left Sunday. I am very weak, kids, lost 15 lbs. Oh well, I could afford that, so that isn't my worry. I do hope Liz is taking care of herself. Let us know as soon as the baby is born.

Ruthie's baby, Issa, is so sweet. Dave [Mudavanha] came over twice while I was in the hospital, and I sure was glad to see him. He looks good, as always. Tell Liz's mom and dad that I got their card and will write when I feel better.

Love Ya! Mother

On January 22, 1978, Ruth gave birth to her second daughter, Issa. Since we were now down two members, we decided to cut back our schedule to concentrate on the children. As we discussed the future of the group and what direction it would take, we decided it was time to completely dispense with the 1940s nostalgia and go in a contemporary direction. We were also able to give Mom and Dad a trip to Hawaii, their first trip out of the continental US, just before our money began to run out.

For us, that was a time of struggle as we tried to decide where to take our careers. Of course, Mother was observing everything we were going through.

November 3, 1979:
Hi Kids,
At this writing I am doing well; had a cold a few weeks ago but feeling better now. I received your card yesterday, sure was glad to hear from you, and glad again that things are moving along for you and your little family so well.

I do believe that things are going to get better, but it is very discouraging right now. Week before last Pastor Small came over with a check from the Church in the amount of $145.00 very much on time. We didn't have any food or money. Oh well, the girls are in L.A. now – did the "Midnight Special," so the next time it appears on the T.V. Guide it will be for real.

This guy Richard Perry is much worse than David (Rubinson); we never had any money problems when they were with David. June is fine and growing up to be a very fine woman.
Love Ya!
Mother

In an attempt to jumpstart our career, we tried to add a third singer in place of June, but Richard said that wouldn't work. Richard told us that if we got June back, he would give us a record deal. No June, no deal. I knew his reputation as a producer who could deliver the hits, and I was determined not to let this opportunity slip through our fingers. We talked to June again, and thankfully she decided to come back. Right away there was a feeling of chemistry and mutual respect. June had already committed to providing guest vocals on our cover of *Sly Stone's* "Everybody Is a Star." After that she officially returned to the group and we were a trio once again. And now we had a record deal. An added incentive for June was that she would be able to record her own album. To make it official that this was a "new" group, we dropped the "The" and became Pointer Sisters.

Richard liked us; he liked where we were from, the work we had done and that we weren't just your ordinary R&B singers who move and dress alike. He loved our style and would even come over to where we lived and pick out things for us to wear for photo shoots and record company parties and the like. He was very involved in everything we did.

After we had a record deal, Richard wanted us to obtain new management. He thought we should be with a high-profile firm and got us signed with Jerry Winetraub, a film producer and talent manager. We were sorry to part with Forrest, but we were willing to do what needed to be done. Our hope was that with his movie connections, Jerry would get our songs, or us, into a movie since we'd already done *Car Wash*.

Things didn't seem to be working out with Jerry, so we switched our management to Gallin Morey, a joint venture with Sandy Gallin and Jim Morey. Sandy was particularly successful having worked with people like Cher, Dolly Parton, Michael Jackson, and Neil Diamond. One of the first gigs we got through him was a chance to play Las Vegas, but there were some issues. First, we were scheduled to play at Caesar's Palace, but they wouldn't give us top billing, which Sandy insisted on. Since he was a good friend of Steve Wynn, he moved our show to the Mirage where we got top billing and more money. We needed that money because one of the stipulations was that we had to fund our own show and then recoup with our show earnings. We were as broke as a joke, so Sandy arranged for us to get a bank loan. That way we could pay famed choreographer Kenny Ortega as well as wardrobe, makeup, and everything else. After that, any time one of their acts like Siegfried and Roy wanted a vacation, we were called to fill in. It was a great venue to play. Also, I made sure that we paid off that loan as fast as possible!

We were learning that Richard could be something of a prima donna at the recording studio. It was his company and his playground. He wanted to live that cliché Hollywood, rock 'n' roll lifestyle. When he was in the studio, he had his hairdresser, and had special food being brought to him; his stack of magazines already had parts highlighted for him to read reports and articles about his clients. He would be going through magazines while we were in there singing.

FIRE

He might look up and say, "Do that again." He was always distracted, and it would piss me off because sometimes what we had done was really, really good, but he hadn't even paid attention. He had his head down in a magazine or he was actually getting his hair cut. I mean he was really playing the role. I think it was that year, 1979, that he had been chosen as Producer of the Year. He once called us in to do background singing for Barbra Streisand on her song "Emotion." (I still have a bracelet she gave me as a gift.) So, we learned to take the good with the bad.

In 1978, we began working on our fifth studio album titled *Energy*, and this one had a totally different vibe from our previous work. Richard acted as producer and he wanted a more laid-back, Southern California sound. The ten songs that made the cut, with some amazing writers, were: "Lay It on the Line," "Dirty Work," written by Walter Becker and Donald Fagen, "Hypnotized" by Bob Welch, "Come and Get Your Love" by Russ Ballard, "Happiness" by Allen Toussaint, "Fire," written by Bruce Springsteen, "Angry Eyes" by Kenny Loggins and Jim Messina, "Echoes of Love," and "Everybody is a Star."

The first single was a cover of Bruce Springsteen's "Fire." Richard had played the song for us and asked me to sing it. I thought the register was too low for me. Maybe it was better suited for Ruthie, but he insisted. We trusted his guidance and he was right. We also went to a club in LA and made a performance video for the song. That was before MTV and they were called in-house videos, not music videos, and they were mostly used for promotion.

"Fire" was a smash hit for us, climbing to the number 2 spot on the *Billboard Hot 100* in February of 1979. The song reached number 1 around the world including Belgium, the Netherlands, South Africa, and New Zealand. It was also a hit in Australia, Austria, Canada, Germany, and the UK. We'd had gold albums before, but this was our first gold single. That song really made a difference in our career and set us up nicely to take over the pop charts. The album *Energy* reached number 13 on the US album chart.

As we enjoyed our success, we were happy that Bonnie was doing the same. She had met a man named Jeffrey Bowen, who was the number one producer at Motown, having created hit records for DeBarge, Honey Cone, The Commodores, and Rick James. Bonnie worked with Jeffrey on her first solo album and Berry Gordy was the

Executive Producer. Bonnie told me that Jeffrey said he was going to make her bigger than Diana Ross.

While we were working on our album with Richard Perry, Jeffrey would say things like: "You guys are not going to do anything working with that white man. He can't do nothing for nobody. Bonnie's goin' to blow up!" I understood that he was supporting his new artist, and we wanted Bonnie to succeed, too, but it wasn't a competition by any means.

Bonnie said, "My *Bonnie Pointer* first album was also called *The Red Album*. I had planned to make a rainbow of album covers. You know: purple, yellow, so that people when they came into a record store – remember those? Could easily recognize my albums by color. It really was not that important to me to be Bonnie Pointer and not a Pointer Sister, not at all. It may have been important to others, but not to me. Crazy me, I wanted it all: I wanted both. Why not? So, it was more important to my sisters than it was to me."

On that solo album, the Brian Holland/Lamont Dozier's "Heaven Must Have Sent You" became a disco hit for Bonnie reaching Number 11 on the *Billboard Hot 100*. The song had first been performed back in 1960 by The Elgins. Bonnie had suggested to Berry Gordy that he have her remake the song as a disco track after she heard the Village People's smash hit "YMCA" and realized that "Heaven Must Have Sent You" would work well with a similar arrangement. She was right.

Bonnie wanted to record other Motown tunes, "simply because I've always dug them." Then there was the controversial song "Free Me from My Freedom." This song made a lot of people angry when it hit the airwaves. Sadomasochistic literalists with visions of a woman demanding her lover to "tie me to a tree, handcuff me" were too much for "liberated women" who didn't pause to listen to the rest of the lyrics. In the 1980 *Jet* magazine article, "Bonnie Pointer: Freedom is Good but Love is Better," Bonnie conceded that full equality for women was a valid goal and that the song wasn't to be taken literally. But I'm sure she knew it would stir up some controversy.

"I had some feedback from people on the radio who wouldn't play it. Yeah, some stations wouldn't play it, but that's where their heads were. They thought I was being masochistic or something, that's where their minds were. But I was seeing a wholly different story. So, it caused a little commotion, but if they can't deal with it, they just can't deal with themselves—period. I didn't see what could be so wrong. I wasn't thinking about getting tortured or anything like that. I was just trying to make a point and to stress that point strongly. Coming from a family of two ministers, I learned how to just push a point across. Each song I've written, I have had to put myself into a different mood to do that song because they were all saying something different."

For her second self-titled album, known as *The Purple Album* (1979), Bonnie recorded "I Can't Help Myself " (Sugar Pie Honey Bunch) first done by the Four Tops, and "Nowhere to Run (Nowhere to Hide) by Martha and the Vandellas, two more Holland-Dozier-Holland Motown classics of the 1960s. Jeffrey Bowen, now Bonnie's husband, also produced that album.

"One reason I married Jeffrey was because he asked me to. He was the first guy to ever ask me to marry him. After the release of my second album, we toured all over Europe: England, Germany, France, and Spain. I was number one in Mexico for six months. This was during the '80s. I traveled with a band and had some of the best musicians in the world. I had a superstar band and I was a superstar. I've done cruise ships. I did a Carnival Cruise for a month. We went to Cozumel; we went to Puerto Rico. It was a gay cruise. I was in their closets every day. I didn't have to be worried about being hit on; they were all gay; I could wear their clothes. It was really fun. I was like RuPaul."

"The gay community's love of The Pointer Sisters," Bonnie said, "comes from the fact that we're real. We come straight...straight outta Oakland. The Pointer Sisters—me, June, and Anita—were bridesmaids at the first gay wedding in San Francisco, when Sylvester married his lover in Golden Gate Park. I spoke with Sheryl Lee Ralph recently and she's doing a play about Sylvester, a Broadway play called *Mighty Real*. People may wonder what happened to me. Well, I'm working. I love this business. I love this life. There's no business like...you know the rest."

Bonnie understood that the legitimization of violence against homosexuals and Jews and women and blacks came from the belief that the Bible condemned these people, so it was okay to attack them. In the late 1970s, Bonnie, in fact, had a gay boyfriend, Daniel Mendez, and they lived together—with Daniel's boyfriend, in a beautiful flat in San Francisco, in the Fillmore District. Dad had introduced Daniel—

tall and lean, with thick black curly hair—to her after a show in San Francisco. "Dad really liked Daniel, who had a very opposite, macho twin brother, and Dad thought Daniel was the nicest guy. And, he was right. My only requirement was that he not embarrass me in public...kissing and holding hands with him and all that...when I'm with them."

So, Daniel reminded Bonnie, in more ways than one, that "Adam and Eve were not the end of the story," and he said to her once, "There's nothing in The Story—with a big 'S'—about friendship or just staying single." Bonnie bragged, "Daniel was fine, handsome, intelligent, and humble." Another time he said to her, "I believe egotistical, lazy, greedy, and mean people are a more serious problem than whom I sleep with. These rules and codes, in the Old Testament, could not have been written by a non-material, spiritual being, but by some dude; a Jewish dude, writing for Jewish people, a long time ago, when they wanted to create more Jews and try to be different from the people around them. So, for Jews, at that time, any sexual activity that interfered with the possible birth of the Messiah was null and void. Masturbation or any 'sex' not to make a baby, null and void. Well, I'm not Jewish and I'm not living two thousand years ago. I think love is where you find it."

Bonnie, who by the way never had children and can't say if she ever *really* wanted children, confesses: "You know, back then, in the '70s, I really didn't know what being gay really meant. We just loved each other, Daniel and me. Love was where you found it. Love was in the heart. I sometimes had a girlfriend stay with me. You know, sometimes you feel like a nut, sometimes you don't. We just loved each other and took care of each other. I loved to cook; she loved to clean. We made love, sometimes the two of us, sometimes three of us. Back then, we didn't know about AIDS, just love and living."

Sadly, that horrible epidemic started in the mid-to-late 1970s. By 1980, HIV may have already spread to five continents (North America, South America, Europe, Africa and Australia). Then, in 1981 there were reports of a group of young men in New York, Los Angeles, and San Francisco with an unusually aggressive cancer named Kaposi's Sarcoma. In the mid-80s, Daniel and his lover would be among the first victims of HIV/AIDS. Bonnie, after being tested, had long since moved on and was married to Jeffrey Bowen.

FIRE

There were also health issues in our own family. In June of 1979, Mother called Fritz and Aaron and the girls, and told them "Daddy's dying." We'd heard this before, but this time there was something in the timbre of Mother's voice that said, "no hope." The desperateness of her revelation shook whatever foundation we thought was under us...gripped us with the futility of a man reaching for a rope of sand. "He was in a coma for more than an hour," Mother said to Fritz. "The girls are comin' up from Hollywood. I don't know about Bonnie. I called Aaron, he's comin' down from Tacoma.

"The girls said they'd have a ticket waiting for you at the airport. The travel agent is going to call to get your itinerary. You just have to tell 'em when you gon' come. They said they'll pay for Liz, too, whenever she's ready."

Dad was at the Novato Convalescent Hospital during his last days. His soft breathing was unnerving, but appreciated, even welcomed as we looked at each other with awkward, distorted smiles, then moved forward into the medicinal chamber. To the right side of Dad's bed was some kind of resuscitative machine, with buttons and dials and hoses, curling from a rectangular tank, like the plastic tentacles of a metal, baby octopus. We were all there, at the family home in Novato, together when Daddy died on June 9, 1979. He was 78.

An overflow crowd of hundreds whose lives he had touched attended his funeral service in Oakland, at our home church, renamed the 23rd Avenue Church of God. Bonnie, now a hit solo act, and her husband, Jeffrey Bowen, the Motown Producer, sent word to the family that, "Bonnie doesn't have time for all this. How much money do you want? That's all you want anyway. We'll send the money." Our collective answer was: "No thanks. We don't need your money."

It was a beautiful service: June, Ruth, and I sang, Uncle Jack sang, the choir sang and the eulogy by our dear family friend, Aubrey LaBrie, could not have been more appropriately eloquent. He spoke of our father as "the founder and leader of our extended family...the chief of our tribe."

He said:

The extended family is an idea that I began to appreciate as I grew in the knowledge of relationships as very important. This was true before we left Africa. And it has also been true of our experience in America. Our strong sense of family helped us endure the burden of slavery and provided support for us when we left the small towns in the South in order to come to the big cities of the North. As you no doubt have already guessed, extended family means more than just our small, immediate families. It also means, in this case, the combination of all our families who met regularly at 10th and Myrtle Streets in order to worship, socialize, and engage in good, old-time fellowship under the guidance of Rev. Pointer, Our Leader and the Chief of Our Tribe.

As we rose from our pews that day, grasping hands and arms, Aaron and Fritz on either side of mother; Ruth, June, and I holding each other as we walked the middle aisle of the church, holding up Mother as she wept profusely. Then she cried out: "I tried! I tried! Elton, I tried to be a good wife...a good mother...I tried, Elton...I tried."

Chapter 11

HE'S SO SHY

N 1980, WE WERE ALL SEARCHING FOR OUR NEW NORMAL. BONNIE was enjoying her successful solo career, we were working on a new album and getting back on track as Pointer Sisters, and the family was trying to adjust to a life without Dad. As usual, Mother captured our feelings at the time in one of her letters to Fritz.

February 1, 1980:

Hello Children,

I am doing okay. Received your letter today and the check. Thanks so much. Oh, I also got the beautiful picture of Mother; thanks so very much. These things mean so much to me. Rose is home. She had an operation and will be home for six weeks. The girls left today for London and Paris, etc., and will be gone for two weeks.

I have my license for my daycare. They came through yesterday. So, I will be trying to get some children real soon. I don't really feel up to it, but I have just got to get some money for myself. I have bills that I made that I am trying hard to pay off.

Well, anyway the Lord is blessing our church and we are glad about this. Thanks again, and I love you very much. Yes, I saw Bonnie too, on this music awards show. She did look real good.

Love to Shegun and Somori and Kiss Liz and the kids for me.

Love Ya,

Mother

To take advantage of the momentum we had created by the hit single "Fire," we began working on our seventh studio album with Richard Perry. The album was titled *Special Things* and once again, we were off in another musical direction, and it turned out to be a smart move.

Instead of rock n' roll songwriters, Richard turned to some of the top pop music lyricists of the day to provide material including Carole Bayer Sager and Burt Bacharach, Bill Champlin, Tom Snow and Cynthia Weil. Richard pushed us into pop music territory because he was sure that after the success of "Fire," we could really make a mark in that genre. We were always ready for a new challenge, and with our revamped group, it was the perfect time to take a chance.

For the album cover, we were more stripped down, literally. Our hair and makeup were minimal, we wore outfits that definitely signaled the 1980s era, but they were not like the flashy gowns we had become known for. We wanted our image to shine through as a trio of women ready to take on the pop world. The nine tracks that ended up on the album were "Could I Be Dreaming" (I wrote the lyrics), "He's So Shy," "The Love Too Good to Last" by Bacharach, Sager, and Peter Allen, "Evil," "Save This Night for Love," "We've Got the Power," "Where Did the Time Go," another Bacharach/Sager song, "Here Is Where Your Love Belongs," and "Special Things" (a song which I wrote, but the record company did not release as a single even though it was the title cut of the album).

The hit streak that started with "Fire" continued when "He's So Shy" hit the Top Five on the pop charts. I knew when I heard it that it would be a hit song. I liked the fact that it was a great follow-up to "Fire," but I did have some initial reservations. The song was initially titled "She's So Shy" and planned for Leo Sayer, but Richard had a different plan. He changed the song to "He's So Shy" and June sang lead. I was a bit apprehensive because it was reminiscent of songs from the '50s like "He's So Fine" which was a style we were moving away from, but I trusted Richard and the process.

I'd initially wanted to sing lead on that song, but Richard thought June's voice worked better and I understood. After all, we had been making compromises throughout our career, and ultimately, I wanted what was best for the group because then we all benefitted. I was able to write the title song and contribute to the opening track, so things worked out. "He's So Shy" became gold-certified, hitting the number 3 spot on the *Billboard Hot 100* and *Cash Box*. It went to number 10 on *Hot R&B/Hip-Hop*, number 13 on *Adult Contemporary*, and 26 on the *Dance Club Songs* chart. We even sang the song on an episode of the popular TV show *The Love Boat* in 1981 which co-starred our high school friend Ted Lange.

Richard was a great music producer. He was a drummer back in his youth and played with a couple of bands. He was good at mixing and arranging the music, but he also allowed us to arrange our own vocals. When we got with Richard, it put us in a whole new category. With "Fire" being a single hit, it took us to someplace we had never been. It was a whole different feeling. I didn't know how powerful a single was: not an album, just a single. We had a gold album with David Rubinson, but never a single. Radio stations all over the world were playing that single, but they're not gonna play a whole album. That's why the hit single became so important for us. The album *Special Things* reached number 19 on the *Billboard Top R&B/Hip-Hop Albums* and number 34 on the *Billboard 200*.

September 4, 1981

Dear Fritz, Liz, Shegun, Nandi and Somori:

How are you all today? At this writing, we are all fine—looking forward to school opening Tuesday. Everybody seems to be looking forward to going back to school, even Faun. Issa is fine and she asks about Nandi every day. I didn't realize that she was so attached to Nandi. I sure miss my Nandi, too.

The girls are in Europe and will be home on the 10th—or should I say will be back in the United States and will be going on to Chicago for two weeks. They want me to meet them in Chicago with Issa. I guess I will try to do just that, if I can't get Faun or Malik to go. Or, they would just drop-off Issa and stay Sat. and Sun. and come back for school Monday.

We are in a "Revival" at our church: Dr. Benjamin Reed is our guest speaker, and he is very good.

I do hope that Nandi is enjoying school. Liz and Fritz, I want to say "thanks" again for a beautiful summer. I have told everyone how wonderful you both were to me and Issa. The children are so happy to have me home. My daycare parents are, too. I have four daycare children already. How is Somori? Does he miss me?

Well dear, again thanks for a wonderful summer, and remember, I love you very much.

Mother

Pointer Sisters were enjoying our success with "He's So Shy," and we were excited about the new direction. More importantly, we were energized by the reception from fans old and new. I could feel our career heating up and knew that this was no time to pat ourselves on the back. In the music industry, if too much time passes between hits, it can be detrimental to a career. I was not about to let that happen. Also, with June re-engaged in the group, I wanted to make sure we made the most of this opportunity.

In 1981, we recorded our eighth studio album titled *Black & White*. Richard stayed with the same tone of the last record, strategically building first on "Fire" and then "He's So Shy." This was yet another piece of the puzzle as we continued our takeover of the pop music charts. The album had nine songs: "Sweet Lover Man," "Someday We'll Be Together," "Take My Heart, Take My Soul," "Slow Hand," "We're Gonna Make It" (with writing credits to me, June, and David Foster), "What A Surprise" (also by June and me), "Got to Find Love," "Fall in Love Again," and "Should I Do It." June and I sang most of the leads, me on four songs and her on six. Of course, the smash hit was the song "Slow Hand." Richard said he knew it would be a hit and thought it was the perfect complement to our previous chart toppers. I sang the lead on "Fire," and Richard decided I should do it on "Slow Hand" as well.

Everything fell into place as we had all hoped. The song was a huge hit reaching the number 2 spot on *Billboard Top 100* and *Cash Box*, number 6 on *Adult Contemporary*, and number 7 on *Hot R&B/Hip-Hop Songs*. Around the world the song was in the top 10 in Australia, Canada, Ireland, New Zealand, South Africa, and the UK. The track had a decidedly country feel and was later even covered by Conway Twitty.

During this time, we were also venturing into the world of music videos that were popularized by MTV's debut in 1981. Soon, music videos were a requirement for any act in the 1980s that wanted to stay on the charts. We had filmed videos previously. The one for "He's So Shy" was low-budget and not very creative, but I enjoyed the process and saw that this would be a new way to reach our audience besides attending live shows or seeing us on TV. The video for "Slow Hand" was stripped down, just the three of us in soft pastel-colored silk robes in front of a roaring fire. The gauzy focus fit the song as we sat on a white rug with instructions to just keep singing to the camera, which we did, as it rotated above, shooting us from every angle.

The next release was the song "Should I Do It" in the spring of 1982 with June singing lead. That song had an interesting history, because it was yet another one with a country music crossover. Tanya Tucker recorded the song the same year we did, but the pop slant of our version had more success. The song went to number 13 on the *Billboard Hot 100* and number 19 on *Adult Contemporary*.

With two Top Twenty hits, the album *Black & White* was certified Gold in September 1981, reaching number 13 on the *Billboard 200* album chart and number 9 on *Top R&B/Hip Hop Albums*. We were fully in the pop area with "Slow Hand" becoming one of our signature songs. Every track on that album had the right mix of a nod to our past and a look toward our pop future. It really felt that as the Pointer Sisters trio, we had found our groove.

Things were looking up for us and of course Mother was watching with maternal pride as we continued to follow the family creed: "When I'm blessed, you're blessed." We were back on our feet again, making good money, and charting songs. To celebrate, we decided to take Mother with us to Europe, specifically Rome and Milan. This time when Mother wrote to Fritz, she used stationary from the Hotel Leonardo Da Vinci.

Hi Kids,

Rome is out of sight! I still can't believe that I'm here. But I am!! I'm having a great time. The Girls have gone downstairs to do TV tapes. Oh, I've never been so happy. Didn't think I would ever get a trip like this, but here I am, in Rome, Italy! We are staying at the Leonardo Da Vinci Hotel. So far, the weather is super, very nice, like California.

Issa was very good the whole trip, so far. The flight was long. We were all day and night on TWA. I thought the service was nice, but what do I know? The Girls were upset about the service, said it was the worst that they had ever had (smile).

We leave Wednesday for Milan, then Brussels, then Paris. From Paris, Issa and I will leave The Girls and fly back home.

Love Ya!

Mother

While touring in support of the *Black & White* album, I was surprised to find that female fans in particular had developed a real affinity for the song "Slow Hand" and its message of female pleasure and empowerment. It became something of a female anthem because of its message, which I had intentionally delivered in a seductive manner as a way to appeal to listeners while also sending a message. The song title became a call for female equality in the bedroom and beyond, urging lovers to "spend some time," one with "an easy touch" who would put a higher value on teasing anticipation and gradual sensation than on mechanically grinding body parts.

The fact that the song was written by two male songwriters, John Bettis and Michael Clark, didn't matter because it was all about the amazing lyrics and singing with sincerity and conviction. It worked perfectly with my voice, and it made me proud that it became such a cultural phenomenon.

February 22, 1982
Dear Liz and Fritz
How are you and the children today? We are fine. I am here in Lake Elsinore, California: "the valley of the drunks." Ha, Ha. I will be here until Thursday. Then, I go over to San Bernardino for a women's convention. I will speak there Thursday and Friday night; then, back home to the workplace. Leon (Mother's brother) is at the house while I am away. Rose and Issa are with me.
I am sending $15.00 to Somori; $10.00 to Shegun; $5.00 to Nandi; total $30.00. Tell the kids that I love them very much. The Girls are fine; they will go to the Grammy Awards Wednesday night.
Love ya. Somori, have a good Happy Birthday
Mother

Rose Gibson was Mother's friend and church-buddy for the past twenty-five or more years; and Mom and Dad's "handy-woman" and chauffeur for the past ten or so. Rose was white and, perhaps to some, a peculiar sight around the Pointer house. When needed, Rose changed the car oil or belts or tires, right in the house garage. If necessary, she unbolted and lifted toilets off the floor to retrieve a doll or stuffed animal clogging the pipes. Though she had her own place in Burlingame, CA, she most often spent the night in Novato. It was very interesting that she felt so dedicated to the family.

Our career began to pick up steam while Bonnie's stumbled. By 1981, Bonnie's success came to a standstill when Bowen and Gordy became involved in a commercial dispute, and Bonnie and Jeffrey left the label. Bonnie had to wait until 1984 when she was signed to

Private I Records. Seen in retrospect, her only Private I album, *If the Price Is Right*, was considered by some to be more ambitious, elaborate, and perhaps even better than her Motown efforts, with vocals contributed by Ruth and me, and two tracks written and produced by Brian Holland.

In the studio with Producer Jeffrey Bowen and vocalist Patricia "Bonnie" Pointer were: John Keane, drums; Tom Keane, synthesizer and keyboards; David Williams, Melvin Ragin, Michael Landau, and Tim Pearce, guitar; John Van Tongeren, keyboards and programmer; and, it seemed, the inevitable Paulinho Da Costa, percussion. Gary Lubow and Jeffrey did the mixing. After a couple of songs for the film *Heavenly Bodies*, no new recordings by Bonnie were released, as Private I lost a distribution deal with CBS and got into legal problems, leaving her again without a contract.

Bonnie said, "I went to rehab for a year, and that saved my life and changed my life. I was hanging out with people who were going nowhere, and I didn't want to go with them. Getting away from them was the first step. I was a newcomer to crack, and even June was ahead of me on this one. I actually turned Jeffrey on to it. I was on crack cocaine for about four years before I went to rehab. The drugs messed up our heads, our thinking. We started spending too much money on it. Jeffrey had gone to a company called Private I and wanted me to go with him; and Berry Gordy wanted me to sign exclusively with him. I decided to stick with my husband."

The tensions and fissures in Jeffrey and Bonnie's marriage began to manifest, as Bonnie said: "He tried to separate me from my family and my friends because that's what you do when you want to control. You try to separate people from their friends and family. I didn't like that. I wasn't accepting that. And I didn't have it. Now, we were married for twenty years; and I was faithful, and I was monogamous. You want to know how I left Jeffrey? We were in a hotel in Hollywood. He started one of his usual arguments. So, I said, 'I'm going to go down the hall and get some ice.' I never came back. I got in a limo and never looked back. That's how it ended."

In 1982, it was a new year, and time for more music. This would be our ninth studio album. Once again, Richard came through for us. The album only had eight tracks, but one of the songs became a theme song for us. The first single released was a cover of Prince's song "I Feel for You." It was a modest hit for us and would later become a smash for Chaka Khan. I wrote and sang lead on the title track "I'm So Excited" with writing credit also given to June, Ruth, and Trevor Lawrence. That song became an unofficial anthem for us, and it was very popular when it was released in July of 1982, but it would become an even bigger smash later. This time around, the song reached number 30 on the *Billboard Hot 100* and also charted in Australia and Sweden. "See How Love Goes" was intended to be the third single, but its subject matter about a woman planning an affair with her boyfriend's friend was thought to be too controversial and not fitting our image.

The album also featured "All of You," "Heart Beat," "If You Wanna Get Back Your Lady," "Heart to Heart," and "American Music." That record ended up charting at a decent but not outstanding number 59 on the *Billboard 200* and 24 on the *Top R&B/Hip-Hop Albums* chart. Our sound had definitely changed and now reflected the '80s complete with its synthesizers and keyboard programming.

We were churning out albums on a yearly basis, working hard to give the pop audience more songs. I knew we had to keep feeding the machine in order to maintain the popularity that had grown with each album we released. We would finish our promotional tour for one album and go right into the studio to record the next. This is what we had been working so hard to achieve; despite the crushing schedule, we were not going to let this slip through our fingers.

Break Out was our tenth studio album. It was released in November of 1983 and was aptly titled because it was packed with hit singles. We had struck music gold! Taking the '80s sound of *So Excited!* one step further, this record had a more electro-dance feel. The album did so well, in fact, that it was re-released the following year.

For its original release in 1983, the record had these ten tracks: "Jump," "Automatic," "Baby, Come and Get It," "I Need You," "Dance Electric," "Neutron Dance," "Easy Persuasion," "Nightline," "Telegraph Your Love," and "Operator." We had some of the best songwriters in the industry and the hits just kept on coming. For the re-mix that followed in 1984, the song "Nightline" was replaced by our previous hit "I'm So Excited." Richard didn't plan on releasing "I'm So Excited" again as a single, but I lobbied for it and it worked for us.

We had four top ten hits from the album and remix: "Jump (For

My Love)," "Automatic," "Neutron Dance," and once again "I'm So Excited." Then the song "Neutron Dance" was used in the hit film *Beverly Hills Cop* starring Eddie Murphy and it was moving back up the charts. However, at first, we weren't sure if the album would be a hit. The lead single was a mid-tempo song called "I Need You." Richard had hoped it would be picked up on R&B stations, which it was, but it wasn't a crossover hit. The other songs were up-tempo, and fans couldn't get enough of them. "Jump" had June singing lead and it was infectious, going all the way to number 3. "Automatic" wasn't initially planned as a release, but it was discovered by club DJs and played in heavy rotation at nightclubs across the country. That song went to number 5 in the US and number 2 on the R&B charts. "I'm So Excited" was re-released and this time it went to number 9, much higher than when it was first released.

"Neutron Dance" went to number 6, thanks to *Beverly Hills Cop*, and "Baby, Come and Get It" was a minor hit in 1985, reaching number 44 in the *Hot 100* and number 24 in *R&B*. The *Break Out* album sold over three million copies in the US and won two Grammy awards and two American Music Awards.

With the original in 1983 and re-release coming out in 1984, we were on the radio constantly for the next few years. Indicative of the comprehensive scope of Richard's production vision for the album *Breakout* was the awareness that for the ten tracks of the record, he selected seventeen keyboardists and synthesizers to achieve the unique and distinctive sound of those tracks. When I found out there were so many musicians, I was surprised, but it worked for us. My favorite thing about *Break Out* was the fact that the single was included on the re-release, after being overlooked on the *So Excited* album, and that the new music showed how much we had grown as artists. We didn't want to sound like anybody else, and we never have. We really got it together on that record.

Richard said, "We managed to find the secret [of the Pointer Sisters]. We have complete mutual respect and trust. The chemistry has to be there, and it is." *Break Out* was his sixth album with us, more than he had done with any other artist he had worked with. "The most I ever did before with any other artist was three each with Carly Simon and Leo Sayer. I've always wanted the kind of ongoing relationship I have with the Pointers." When he was looking for songs for us, he said his major requirements were "a distinctive melody and a tastefully provocative lyric that exemplifies the feelings of independent young women."

For "I'm So Excited," since I had written the song with Trevor, we were supposed to split the publishing credit (and royalties) 50/50. However, I was getting smarter about the business, and I wanted to share the publishing with Ruthie and June so they would benefit in the revenue. Ultimately, Trevor and I agreed to a 40/60 split so that June, Ruth, and I would get 20% each. I always felt protective of the group and concerned about our financial success. I was taught by Mother to follow the family creed: "If I'm blessed, you're blessed."

Another factor that contributed to the astounding success of "I'm So Excited" was the music video choreographed and directed by Kenny Ortega. He's the same Kenny Ortega who choreographed dances for the film *Dirty Dancing*, as well as Madonna's music video *Material Girl*, and was on board for Michael Jackson's *This Is It* tour before Michael died. We first started working with Kenny when we signed with Richard. Richard said to him, "I've got this new group I'm working with, they have a new record out, you may not have heard of them, and I would like you to work with them: the Pointer Sisters. Do you know who they are?"

Kenny had responded, "Do I know them? Are you kidding? Do I know them? I love the Pointer Sisters and have loved them for a long time. I followed them before they had a hit record."

I was blown away when I heard that he was such a true fan of what we were doing. I think that's why we worked so well with him. He believed in us, and we put our trust in him. I'm still friends with him to this day. He recently told me how much he loved working with us on those videos and the choreography for all of our Las Vegas shows. The video for "I'm So Excited" is a classic that stands the test of time—turning over that table, June in the bathtub, that was really risqué stuff back then. He even introduced us to Debbie Reynolds and took us to rehearse at Debbie Reynolds Dance Studios in the Valley. It has been a wonderful experience and relationship working with Kenny Ortega.

Thanks to input by Kenny and everyone else, *Break Out* was our most successful album and half the songs made it to the Top Ten. That was practically unheard of. The writers of "Neutron Dance,"

Allee Willis and Danny Sembello, had hoped it would be used on the soundtrack of the film *Streets of Fire* because it fit the topic. Allee said, "We were told that there had been this nuclear holocaust, and that a '50s doo-wop black group was going to be at the back of the bus that the lead couple was escaping on..." The song ended up on *Beverly Hills Cop* and everything worked out. *Break Out* continued to stay on the charts even longer than our other records since we put out so many videos and they were all in heavy rotation at MTV.

Because the same album was re-released, though we were busy promoting, that gave us a break at the studio. June took that time to record the solo album she had been promised. In 1983, *Baby Sister*, co-produced by Richard Perry and Norman Whitfield, was released on Planet Records. The single "Ready for Some Action" contributed by none other than Holland-Dozier-Holland reached the Top 30 on the R&B charts. Trevor and I wrote an up-tempo song with June for the album called "New Love, True Love."

True to his word, Richard made sure that she was able to record her own album. I never really doubted it because he was always a big fan of hers. Richard said of June, "She's got a hard, sexy edge to her voice. She's the personification of the Pointer Sisters, and she sang lead on several songs." So, he was sure that she was ready for a solo record. The problem was that with the Pointer Sisters albums coming out so close together, June's work was basically overlooked and did not do as well as it could have. The timing was not right, and in the music business, timing is everything.

June seemed to take it in stride because she was very proud of our hit album. "It's like we were in a laboratory or something," she said. "But in terms of the material, with songs like 'Automatic,' 'I Need You,' 'Easy Persuasion,' and 'Jump,' it's the most personal record we've ever done."

Richard agreed. "It's a positive sound. It was back to the same positive 'up' thing of 'Yes, We Can (Can),' but with the synthesizers, and especially the drum sound we got. It's completely modern."

Not content to just release a solo album, June had some career plans of her own. She performed the song "Little Boy Sweet" for the 1983 film *National Lampoon's Vacation*, starring Chevy Chase. She also posed for *Playboy* magazine that year. In addition to the brutal trauma she had suffered at such a young age and the depression that resulted from that, she had also been diagnosed as bipolar. Then, during this time in her life, she announced that she was also bisexual. She began a relationship with a woman and the family accepted it as a part of life. They obviously loved each other very much, that was apparent, and truly that was the important thing as far as we were concerned.

June and Fritz shared a special bond, not the least of which was being *decade twins*; she was his tenth birthday present. More than once June had called announcing, "Hey Fritz, it's me, June." Her interest in Africa and African people was genuine and sincere. She wanted to know about the conditions and lives of the people there. She wanted to know how white people could be racist in South Africa, a country full of black people. She wondered why white people would go all the way to South Africa if they hated black people. If they hated black people so much, she wondered, why would they move into their country?

She knew that Fritz had visited Africa with Mudavanha: Ghana, Egypt, Tanzania, and Libya in 1984 when it was thriving. Taxis there were Mercedes and people were playing chess and backgammon in beautiful parks. Mudavanha and Fritz were there, along with Dr. Jeremiah Wright (pastor), Sonja Sanchez (poet), Russel Means (AIM), Bob Brown (A-APRP) and Louis Farrakhan (NOI) to celebrate the Libyan Jamahiriya (Revolution). Twenty-seven years later, under Barack Obama, it would be utterly destroyed by American bombs; its leader, Muammar Gaddafi, murdered.

Fritz and Mudavanha had talked with June about their experiences in Africa. How they loved Africa and wanted to return as often as possible. In fact, Mudavanha had been going to Ghana every year for the past twenty years. June longed to go to Africa. Also, in 1984, the Pointer Sisters were invited to appear in Sun City, South Africa. June talked with Dr. Daniel Kunene (Fritz's father-in-law) about the trip.

June said, "What do you think about us playing Sun City in South Africa? I've really been wanting to go to Africa ever since I missed the trip in '74 when Bonnie, Anita, and Ruth went to the Muhammad Ali/George Foreman boxing match in Zaire."

Dr. Kunene responded, "June, I don't think that the Pointer Sisters should play Sun City. It would not be a wise thing or the right thing to do right now. The Apartheid System still exists in South Africa: the same system that sent government-police to murder school children in Soweto. June, the money cannot be worth your soul. Please, look into the organization Artists United Against Apartheid. And please share what I've said with Anita, Ruth, and Bonnie. I know you all will do the right thing."

Because of that sobering conversation, we did not play Sun City. Instead, we became a part of the more than 50 artists representing rock, jazz, reggae, Latin, and African music, including: Bruce Springsteen, Miles Davis, Steven Van Zandt (Little Steven), Afrika Bambaataa, Ruben Blades, Bono, Kurtis Blow, David Ruffin, Bob Dylan, Bonnie Raitt, Darlene Love, Keith Richards, Bobby Womack, and others who joined to protest in song and video: "I...I...I...Ain't Gonna Play Sun City!" in the black, so-called homeland of Bophuthatswana, created by the Apartheid system.

On October 30, 1985, the *Sun City* album was presented to the United Nations. It's so wonderful to know there are people, artists, who put principle over a paycheck, and we were glad to support the cause. The artist royalties from the record, video, and related books were donated to The Africa Fund and used to support political prisoners and their families inside South Africa, the educational and cultural needs of South African exiles, and the educational efforts of anti-apartheid groups in the United States.

Our group had enjoyed steady, gradual popularity in the past, but by the mid-1980s, we were at a new level. June said that people stopped her for autographs when she went to buy toilet paper at her grocery market. "It's not as bad as Michael," she said. "We don't have to wear disguises...I hope it comes to that."

With our skyrocketing popularity, our look was evolving and following the '80s trends. June liked to wear snakeskin shoes, black fishnet stockings, and yellow outfits. Her hair was basically one color until she pulled it up at the back of her head to reveal a streak of blond underneath, a hidden surprise, much like June was. Ruth became a strawberry blond. She dyed part of her hair light red, and then she dyed another part blond. As far as my style, I was putting blue and pink strands into my hair for a dash of color. I usually favored black silk pants, black blouse and black lace socks. I wore a ring from Kenny Rogers, and two bracelets: one from Barbra Streisand and one from Byron Allen who had opened for us at the Kennedy Center.

We had so much fun with a concept video that Kenny choreographed and directed for our song "Dare Me." In it we were dressed as slick businessmen, complete with suits and facial hair. It took place in a boxing gym and we were inspiring a boxer to be his best. It was unlike anything we had done before and we had so much fun. It was creative and challenging and of course filled with Kenny's trademark dance moves. Later in the video we are decked out in shiny dresses with big hair, dancing in the boxing arena as June sang lead.

That song was from our 1985 album called *Contact*. The record also included the songs "Twist My Arm," "Hey You," "Pound, Pound, Pound," "Back In My Arms," "Burn Down the Night," "Bodies and Souls," "Contact," "Dare Me," and "Freedom." The album was certified platinum and we won an American Music Award the next year for Favorite Video Group. "Dare Me" went to number 11 in the US and number 17 in the UK, thanks in part to the innovative video. "Twist My Arm" and "Freedom" were also released. That year, the Showtime premium (cable network) showed the *Pointer Sisters in Paris*, which was taped May 14 and 15 at the Le Rex Concert Hall and simulcast by Westwood One Radio Networks.

We had spent the mid-80s recording an album, touring, promoting, making music videos, and recording again. It was hectic and challenging for all of us, but we were determined to hold onto our hard-earned popularity for as long as we could. We had worked too hard and sacrificed too much to backslide now. It seemed like we had found our groove with Richard and his affinity for pop hits.

I just hoped it would last.

Chapter 12

LOVE FOR WHAT IT IS

HERE'S NO DENYING THAT WE PUT A LOT OF WORK INTO OUR career, particularly in the 1980s, after resurrecting the group when two of my sisters wanted to go in different directions. Fortunately, we were able to pull it all back together. In fact, we purposely omitted lead vocal credits on our albums even though that may have confused fans who wanted to follow us individually and learn more about each sister. It was quite intentional that we be viewed as a group, a cohesive unit, instead of individuals who just happened to sing together. I felt that even though we had our own distinctive looks and personalities, we should consistently present ourselves to the public as the Pointer Sisters. There was no leader.

Working with family can be amazing, but it adds a new layer of difficulty because it's not just about business. It's also about, well, family. As the self-designated mother of the group, I always felt obligated to handle the details and most of the behind-the-scenes work while downplaying my contributions. Even though I did the lion's share of writing and singing lead, I worked hard to attribute everything to the group. There were uncomfortable moments, like when I was chosen to deliver the only speaking line in *Car Wash*, or I was singled out to take center stage in a show or when filming a commercial. "Let's get Anita up front for this shot."

Those times always made me leery because with every accolade I was worried that one of my sisters would think I was trying to outshine them, and that could lead to animosity and dissension. It was tough to stay grounded when everyone around us was singing our praises. Then there were others who whispered in our ear that one of us was the true star. I met lots of people like that. Some seemed genuine and others obviously wanted to get a slice of the Pointer Sisters economic pie. Reaching such heights of fame put all of us to the test. I went into it thinking that as sisters and as a family, we could never be broken, but the reality was quite different.

While I contemplated if and when I should consider my own professional solo moves, I made sure to enjoy the financial rewards of more than a decade of hard work. In 1985, I bought a lot high up in Beverly Hills to build my dream home. It took several years for my dream to be realized, and in 1988, I finally moved in (and still haven't left).

There's no denying that it's a tony area. The gated, hilltop community has boasted a who's who of Hollywood, as its current and former residents include Ed McMahon, Gwen Stefani, Jennifer Lopez, and Damon Wayans. However, I chose the location solely because it was exactly what I had dreamed about, and it was the perfect symbol of all that we had achieved. I'd gone from living in a crowded family house to holing up in a roach-infested Houston home to living in that small apartment in San Francisco writing "Shaky Flat Blues."

Once completed, I couldn't believe how wonderful my dream home had come together. From the upper deck, looking down at the pool, the Jacuzzi to its right gave the structure the shape of a "P" for "Pointer." The home recording studio had an impressive array of state-of-the-art recording, mixing, and special effects equipment so that I could work with other musicians on preproduction versions of our songs, saving expensive studio time and allowing me to stay close to family. The fully equipped private gym with a small lounging area above it was designed with a magnificent racquetball court and speakers carefully placed high on the back wall beyond the ball's usual trajectory. The enormous court was the full height and length of one side of the house: room for a near regulation-size basketball court.

The master bedroom was designed with a completely independent audio-access system to provide immersive sound, with source components mounted flush beside the bar. Downstairs, another audio system, located in the recording studio, fed the entire lower floor, including the patio and racquetball court. There was no denying that this was the home of an entertainer!

As the Pointers Sisters, we were at the top of our game, and it was everything I had imagined. We were headlining and selling out concerts around the world and appearing on TV regularly. Our videos were in high rotations, and we were putting out music yearly to keep our audience satisfied. We were racking up awards as well with three American Music Awards and two Grammys: Best Vocal Arrangement for Two or More Voices ("Automatic") and Best Pop Performance by a Duo or Group with Vocal ("Jump (For My Love").

The night of the 1985 American Music Awards, we had just come off a tour with Lionel Richie and were in a dressing room when someone came running up the stairs and said that several folks wanted to meet us at the A&M Recording Studios after the awards show and the session would include Michael Jackson, Quincy Jones, and Stevie Wonder. It was all very secretive. Earlier that day, we had received a cassette tape with a song on it. We were asked to listen to it and be prepared for an upcoming jam session that would be announced later. We were understandably curious and eager to explore every opportunity, so after the awards show was over, we showed up at the studio. I noticed there was a big sign outside that said, "Leave Your Ego at the Door."

Harry Belafonte, the entertainer and social activist, had started a non-profit foundation called USA for Africa to help feed the starving people of that continent. It was a wonderful symbolic gesture and something we wholeheartedly supported. It was especially important for black entertainers to think of issues bigger than themselves, their egos, and their bank accounts. It was about being able to give back after all of the success we all enjoyed. So, we were glad that they asked us to be a part of what would become a global phenomenon: *We Are the World*.

I knew there were huge talents involved, but I had no idea it was going to be as big as it was. For something so grand, it was incredibly well organized. I suppose with so many moving parts, it had to be. Still, it was amazing to see it all come together. Everyone was advised where to stand and when to sing. Of course, the song was being recorded, and the whole affair was filmed to be released as a music video. The Pointer Sisters initially had a solo part in the song, but it didn't work out because June had to leave early, with Ruthie and me staying to finish the job.

I was standing near Joe Cocker and Latoya Jackson and Sheila E, and we worked all night to finish the song because it would be practically impossible to gather so many superstars in the same room again. There was only one chance to record all the vocals. We didn't get out of there until the next morning, and it was impressive to see how devoted Lionel, Michael, and Quincy were. It was obvious they were determined to get everything right. Always one to live each moment to the fullest, I was not shy about getting everyone to sign the sheet music to commemorate the historic event.

With sales in excess of 20 million copies, the song "We Are the World" was one of the fewer than 30 all-time singles to have sold at least 10 million copies worldwide. The song was awarded numerous honors including: three Grammy Awards, one American Music Award, and a People's Choice Award; it was promoted with a critically received music video, a behind-the-scenes documentary, a special edition magazine, a simulcast, and several books, posters, and shirts. The promotion and merchandise added to the success of "We Are the World" and raised over $63 million (equivalent to $136 million today) for humanitarian aid in Africa and the US.

Quincy Jones said, at the time, that whomever was a part of the session, whether they had solo or lead vocals or not, would forever be a part of a music history milestone. It was a phenomenal night! He was right and I was proud that they asked us to be a part of it. As a self-identified amateur hoarder, I must admit that I still have the "We Are the World" music cassette and the autographed sheet music, because that was a hell of a night. I still can't believe how amazing and wonderful and magical the experience was. We all got together, all the hot artists of 1985: Michael Jackson, Lionel Richie, Quincy Jones, Tina Turner, Bruce Springsteen, everybody—and went into the studio with the same mission. I like to think I spent the night with Michael Jackson and Lionel Richie at the same time. That was incredible: A musical *ménage a trois!*

For most of 1986, we were on the road at any given time, on a US tour that would take us from Caesar's Palace in Vegas (July 15 through 20) to New Jersey's rocking Meadowlands (August 9). We were young, beautiful, and "red hot" as they kept telling us. We did especially well at the casinos where we were a big draw, bringing in large crowds who spent a lot of money; that made everyone happy from coast to coast, especially the casino owners.

Besides "We Are the World," we also participated in other fun side projects. Bruce Willis was just becoming a huge star thanks to his popular role on the TV show *Moonlighting* and his burgeoning movie career. In 1986, we were asked to sing on the song "Respect Yourself," which would be the lead single from his debut album *The Return of Bruno*. June had a lead part in the song, lending music-superstar credibility to the project and helping it to reach the Top Five on *Billboard Hot 100 Singles* chart. She also did an amazing job playing against Bruce in the music video which became one of the most popular clips of that year. June also went on to record a duet with Dionne Warwick called "Heartbreak of Love" for Dionne's 1987 album, *Reservations for Two*. It was part of her continued effort to build her platform as a solo artist.

As our popularity continued to soar, it was time for another album. We couldn't afford to coast along on the success of our hits. We needed to keep them coming. That year saw the release of our twelfth studio album and the eighth collaboration with Richard Perry. The record was titled *Hot Together*. June sang lead vocals on the first single, "Goldmine" (written by Andy Goldmark and Bruce Roberts). Paula Abdul choreographed the accompanying video. The lyrics, so apropos for June, spoke eloquently of appreciating another and being appreciated. The album performed respectably on *Billboard R&B* and *Dance* charts, but only reached #33 on the *Hot 100*. A second single, the ballad "All I Know Is the Way I Feel," only reached #93 on the *Hot 100*. A third release, "Mercury Rising," just managed an appearance on the *Billboard R&B* chart. Unfortunately, "Goldmine" was the only track on the album that came close to the entertainment value of "Dare Me" from *Contact*.

Still, we weren't ready to give up on the album. The title track was well known because it was included in the soundtrack for the Mel Brooks' film *Spaceballs* and the Richard Dreyfuss film *Stakeout*. It was also part of the NBA's late 1980s promotional campaign. Other songs of note included "Set Me Free" (co-written by "Neutron Dance" scribe Allee Willis and featured in the opening scene of Whoopi Goldberg's movie *Jumpin' Jack Flash*) and "My Life" (co-written by actress/comedienne Sandra Bernhard). The album was re-mastered and issued on CD, with bonus tracks, in 2011 by Big Break Records.

While those initial chart rankings would be fine for a newer artist, we were held to a different standard. Because we had cranked out hits that got a lot of attention (and made people a lot of money), we were expected to keep it up; unfortunately, being at the top is practically impossible to maintain. We had been fortunate to ride the wave of pop music, but the trends were changing, as they always do in this industry. New Jack Swing, hip-hop, and grunge were on the rise and taking over the music charts as pop music took a backseat.

I wasn't sure where the Pointer Sisters would go next, and I decided it was time for a few projects of my own. I was so excited about my collaboration with Earl Thomas Conley on the song "Too Many Times" which was released as a single and reached number 2 on the country chart. It was like I was back to my country roots that began with "Fairytale."

My friend Teri Diamond, who was head of RCA, A&R (Artists' Representative) and is still a good friend of mine, came up with the idea that it was time for me to do a solo album. She even offered her husband, Steve Diamond, to play guitar on the record. I loved her idea and her enthusiasm, but I didn't have any material ready. She was determined, and soon she signed up a producer named Preston Glass.

In 1987, I released my project *Love for What It Is.* It felt rushed, and I think the record company was trying to satisfy too many people, but I was proud to put out my own album. The record's first single, "Overnight Success," reached No. 41 on the *Billboard R&B* chart. As that song generated attention, I had to field the Pointer Sisters breakup rumors that I knew would be coming, but I thought anything we did would help the group as a whole.

The album was extra special for me because my daughter Jada, who had made a few appearances with me as a singer, worked with me and received album credit. There are also several songs featuring the backing vocals of Linda "Peaches" Green, of Peaches and Herb fame, and a song called "The Pledge" that I recorded with Phillip Bailey of Earth, Wind, & Fire.

Since June had done her own album, I made sure to talk to her about my album in the dressing room one night, before a show we were playing in Tahoe. June said folks in her camp had told her that I didn't want her doing a solo album. That's exactly what I was talking about when I mentioned how people can get in your ear. I was shocked that she believed something like that without coming to me. She was incredibly upset about my project. I tried to explain that what she had heard was a bullshit lie; I didn't ever say I didn't want her to do a solo album. The only thing I ever said was that I reserved the right to do one as well. In that moment, June slapped me across the face and ran. My frustration got the better of me, and I picked up a bowl of clam dip and threw it at her. The bowl crashed against the door, and the clam dip flew back into *my* face. Everybody laughed, including me. June was mad at me, but I wasn't mad at her. Still, because of that chaos, we had to cancel the show that night. I chartered a private plane and went home to regroup.

That fight of ours in the dressing room was a real wakeup call for me. I fully understood how easy it was for others to get us to turn on each other. It was sobering to realize that our tight union could be so easily compromised. We had always discussed that we would support each other, and everyone was encouraged to pursue other opportunities as long as we came together for the group. It was somewhat ironic that we fought about solo albums because I really didn't like doing the project without my sisters. I couldn't even have any of them sing with me because it was intended to show my talents alone. I did manage to get the kids—Jada, Faun, Malik, and Fritz's son, Shegun and daughter, Nandi— to come to the Record Plant in Sausalito and sing on the song "Have A Little Faith in Love." The one really exciting part of my album was when I performed by myself on *The Arsenio Hall Show*. A review in the *Chicago Tribune* said, "The album leaves you feeling happier, stronger, and wiser for the experience."

On a personal level, things were in flux when my grandmother, Roxie Silas, died at the Novato Convalescent Hospital. Interestingly, according to the local newspaper, *The Novato Advance*, the hospital was issued a citation following the death of Roxie Silas, who was deaf, mute, and blind with both legs amputated. "Silas may have smothered to death when she was trapped between the bars on the side of her bed and couldn't turn over," the newspaper stated. It was possibly an accident, subsequent to the age-related natural disease process. It could also have been a coronary or a stroke. The coroner said Grandma Roxie died from "apparent asphyxia and organic brain syndrome."

No matter how it happened, it was still a blow to the family even though she had been in a vegetative state and hadn't recognized anyone in ten years. So, plans had been made to take Grandma Roxie back to Prescott, Arkansas to be buried next to her companion of sixty years, Granddaddy Fritz. Our roots are deep in the soil of Arkansas, especially Prescott. Grandma Roxie and Granddaddy Fritz lived there for more than sixty years. Our mother, Sarah, grew up there. Our uncles, Leon and "Jack" grew up there. Our cousins, Bill, Leon, and Paul spent a few formative years there. Bonnie and I had attended school there. Our mother and father were married there on July 20, 1941, at 201 Green Lawn Street.

Mother, Uncle Leon, Sister Lee, and Fritz were "chosen" by the family to attend services in Prescott. Uncle Leon praised "The Girls" (as the family referred to the Pointer Sisters) for our generosity. "The girls have paid for five air-trips for me: three to Prescott, one to Chicago, and one to Akron, Ohio. These tickets," he exclaimed, "to Little Rock cost $4,800...first class. I'm The Girls' ambassador for the family."

We were always happy to help out the family, and I was often amused by their reactions. The entrepreneur, always counting the money, Uncle Leon said, "Ten thousand dollars," and he repeated it over and over! "That's what the trip to Prescott cost. When you consider four first-class tickets at thirteen hundred dollars each, the rental car, motel, food, funeral costs—the trip cost ten thousand dollars! Paid for by the Pointer Sisters. I could never thank them enough."

Naturally, we could not attend. We had to work. There was no rest for us, especially with our last album not performing as well as we'd hoped. In 1987, we filmed a special for the NBC network called *Up All Night*. The concept was that after we'd finished our concert tour, we missed our flight and went out on the town in Los Angeles, performing and meeting celebrities along the way. First, we met up with Whoopi Goldberg and we all sang "Can't Get Next to You," a song made famous by the Temptations. Then we sang two songs with Bruce Willis, both from his solo album, "Respect Yourself" and "Texas Woman Blues," which was a cover of a Taj Mahal song. That song came about because we sang backup on the original and Bruce wanted the same backup singers. It was just that now we were singing out in front! That same year, we also performed the song "Santa Claus Is Coming to Town" for the Special Olympics charity album *A Very Special Christmas*. Others on that record included The Eurythmics, Whitney Houston, Bruce Springsteen, Run-D.M.C., and Madonna.

LOVE FOR WHAT IT IS

Serious Slammin' was the title of the album we put out in 1988. By that time, we had recorded fourteen albums in fifteen years, which shows how prolific and determined we were. We realized that with our songs slipping on the charts, movie soundtracks helped to continue the longevity. So, the first single, "He Turned Me Out," was featured in the movie *Action Jackson* starring Carl Weathers, Sharon Stone, and Prince protégé Vanity. It reached number 40 on the R&B chart. We had another modest success with the single "I'm in Love" which made it to number 67. Then there was "Moonlight Dancing" written by Diane Warren, "I Will Be There," and the title track.

We attempted to change up our sound, going in a more R&B and urban direction. Of course, it was a gamble, but we had to give it a shot. We brought on new writers and producers, hoping to capture a new sound. I think we tried to accomplish too much with that record. We wanted to hold on to our old fans and appeal to new ones. We worked hard on every song and gave it our best, doing what I think is some of our best singing. Maybe that record was trying too hard and should have focused on one type of music. It's not easy to look at a personal project like that objectively.

In 1989, June released her second album simply titled *June Pointer* on Columbia Records. It was executive-produced by hit-maker Carol Bayer Sager, and the first single was a song called "Tight On Time (I'll Fit U In)" which went to number 70 on the R&B chart. Irene Cara (known for the movie *Fame*) sang background vocals on "Keeper of the Flame" and Ruth also handled background duties on two songs.

With June's solo album and the latest offering from the Pointer Sisters failing to create a lot of interest, I was unsure what was in store for us as a group...and as a family.

Chapter 13

RIGHT RHYTHM

AS THE POINTER SISTERS, WE HAD AN INTERESTING HISTORY WITH Motown. First off, they passed on signing us as a group when we were looking for our first record deal. Next, after Bonnie left the group, she was signed to Motown until 1981. We also had friendships with a lot of people on the Motown roster even though we worked hard to distance ourselves from some of their girl groups in an effort to establish our own identity; not to mention that Ruth was married to a member of The Temptations, who recorded for the label.

So, I was surprised as anyone when we signed with them to release our 1990 album (our fourteenth studio record) called *Right Rhythm*. I co-wrote the title cut, but again unfortunately, it wasn't released as a single. We separated from Richard Perry because after many albums, there was no question that it was time for a change. We had tried everything we could think of to get back on track with Richard, but nothing worked. Motown was also searching for new artists since its stable of stars were not producing the hits they once did. Looking back, maybe that wasn't the best pairing. We needed hits and so did they. At least we had a singular goal in mind.

The good part of the deal was that we were allowed to act as executive producers on the album (and received credit for that). The bad part was that we didn't receive much support in the way of promotional budget, advertising, or anything else needed to reach the fans. Instead, we were forced to spend our own money to promote as much as we could. The album had a distinctive hip-hop, street sound mixed with our harmonies. I thought it was a solid record and the first single backed that up. "Friends' Advice" reached number 36 on the R&B charts, outperforming some of our previous singles. I hoped this was a sign that things were looking up. The second single was a ballad called "After You," and that one did not do well. Next there was a remixed version of "Insanity," and that one managed to eke out a number 60 on R&B, but did better at number 11 on the *Billboard* dance charts

Switching labels had been a gamble that did not pay off. We had to promote the album with our own finances. When it didn't do well, it was a real let down for us, but we weren't giving up. We made a switch to SBK records and in 1993 released an album titled *Only Sisters Can Do That*. We paired up with producer/songwriter Peter Wolf, who had worked with Starship, Patti LaBelle, Heart, and many others. We had moved from our partnerships with David Rubinson and Richard Perry to putting our hopes into Peter's very capable hands.

I wrote several songs on the album with all three of us writing the title track. The first single released was the song "Don't Walk Away" featuring the talented Michael McDonald (from the bands The Doobie Brothers and Steely Dan) as a guest vocalist. Then there was "It Ain't a Man's World," a song that even included poetry from Maya Angelou, and "I Want Fireworks." Our effort received good reviews including one from *Entertainment Weekly* calling it "the catchiest Sisters set since 1984's hit-packed *Break Out*."

Again, we had tried hard to give the fans what we thought they would like, but what we did not know was that our new label was experiencing challenges of their own and would soon cease to exist. Once again, we were forced to re-evaluate our next steps as a group after such an illustrious history.

For over two decades, from 1973 to 1994, we had recorded and released a total of twenty-three albums, an amazing feat for any artist or group. Naturally, it had all been a labor of love, and we weathered the ups and downs, no matter how insurmountable. We had followed our father's words of wisdom: "If a task is once begun, never finish 'til it's done; be your labor great or small, do it well or not at all." I decided that maybe it was time to think differently. With the popularity of singles, it was no longer necessary to release an entire album, which was an older strategy used to make more money off the strength of one or two songs. We needed to look for other opportunities to perform and reach new audiences. Besides, I had become a grandmother, and my sisters were either divorcing or remarrying, so we had other distractions that we hadn't been faced with when we were devoting all of our time to touring and recording.

In 1991, we were asked by Bob Hope to travel to the Persian Gulf to perform for the troops. It was an honor and we eagerly said yes! In 1994, MCA came up with the concept of pairing country acts with R&B artists for an album called *Rhythm, Country & Blues*. We were asked to record with country hitmaker Clint Black on Aretha Franklin's "Chain of Fools." This project was close to my heart because of my history with country music. I love the idea that there isn't a world of difference between country and soul, something I've been saying for a long time. The producers, Don Was and Tony Brown, came up with a group of 11 duets featuring pairings including Vince Gill and Gladys Knight, Al Green and Lyle Lovett, Little Richard and Tanya Tucker, and Patti LaBelle and Travis Tritt. It was an early precursor to today's trend of country songs infused with hip-hop like "Old Town Road" with Lil Nas X and Billy Ray Cyrus.

It was a beautiful concept and it came at the perfect time for us. "Chain of Fools" was right up our alley and had already been in our repertoire for years. We got along so well with Clint that we recorded the song in no time. It was also filmed for a TV special to air on PBS. That album was a hit, going platinum, and the song we did was nominated for a country music award for Song of the Year. The song was also a top ten hit on the Pop charts, where we had not made a real impact in several years.

The same year that song came out, we were bestowed with the honor of having a star dedicated to us on the Hollywood Walk of Fame. It was a huge event with fans gathered all around us. The town officials proclaimed it "Pointer Sisters Day" in Hollywood. We also had signed with new managers, the firm of Sterling/Winters. With a new team, they were able to open us up to yet another untapped audience as we played opera houses and huge shows overseas including a 20,000-seat arena in Belgium where we sold out ten nights in a row. With their guidance, we now had a successful country hit, a star in Hollywood, and a growing overseas audience. When we returned from Europe, they even had a motorcade escort for us to the American Music Awards where we had been booked to open the show. It was amazing and I felt like we were in a presidential procession! We were only the second female group to receive such an honor. The first was The Supremes.

RIGHT RHYTHM

We had finally found management that not only understood us, but they had been fans of our music before we signed with them, so they were truly invested in our success, which was an amazing feeling. They continued to find new venues for us. In 1995, we signed up for a national tour of the hit musical *Ain't Misbehavin'* which included cast members Eugene Barry-Hill and Michael-Leon Wooley. The show ran for 48 weeks and RCA Records released an album of highlights from the show, which we recorded in one day. They had all the tracks down and we just went in and sang every song just like we were performing a show.

Let me tell you the touring schedule was rigorous and inflexible: eight shows a week, travel on the off days, and interviews and press sandwiched in between. It felt like we'd gone back to our roots because there we were wearing feather boas and platform heels, just like in the old days. While it was an amazing opportunity, it was the hardest thing I have ever done in my life: eight shows a week, with a cast of five. It was not like it was some big ensemble where you can slack off a little bit because somebody else could take over that night and fill in for you. With three women and two men, we were the whole show. There was no day any of us could slack up, and it was so hard to do eight shows a week and sing our best every night. June ended up missing many of the shows, and her understudy had to jump in. I think it was just too much for June to keep up with that hectic pace.

On our days off we were traveling to the next town and doing interviews for the upcoming shows. Jason Winters, thinking of our legacy, had put all this together and encouraged us to do it. He had connections in theater and got us guaranteed money. He wanted us to be part of the history of this iconic musical play, and he was right. It was a great opportunity.

We did 46 weeks from '95 to '96. I understood why June couldn't handle much of the schedule. I thought I was going to lose my mind. I swear, I had no idea how intense and exhausting that type of work is. I gained a whole new appreciation for those who do it all the time. With June sitting out most shows, Ruth and I had a tense, strained relationship during the production.

Then there were all those rules. You had to stick strictly to everything that was the original script...nothing ad lib. It was too tight and closed and rigid: you had to stand in the exact same spot by the piano, sing the exact same note the exact same way. I wished it could have been taped, but that's against theater rules because they want people to come out to the theater. I understood that, but it was such an amazing production that I would love to see it today.

Theater was an amazing professional experience, and I'm glad I did it, although I'm not sure I'd commit for such a long run again. I started to feel like I was operating on autopilot. If I hadn't had Tupac's "California Love" to listen to, I'm not sure if I would have made it. That music along with Andrae Crouch and Sounds of Blackness gave me life and kept me sane. Those songs about California reminded me of home as we crisscrossed the highways of the United States.

Somehow, while performing in the musical *Ain't Misbehavin'*, we also managed to record "Feel for the Physical" as a duet with Thomas Anders (of the band Modern Talking) for his album *Souled*. To top off 1996, we were one of the featured acts at the closing ceremonies of the 1996 Summer Olympics held in Atlanta.

In the 1990s, we had seen our chart popularity diminish somewhat in the music world, but with new management, we were back in the game. It was invigorating that we had conquered new professional challenges and by the end of the decade, we were back in the spotlight with our star once again shining brightly.

The next decade, the 2000s, was a different story entirely.

Chapter 14

MOTHER

LET'S FACE IT. THE NEW DECADE, THE NEW MILLENNIUM, STARTED with over-hyped fears like the Y2K frenzy and the smoke and mirrors of internet IPOs. The end wasn't much better. By 2010, the United States had experienced a devastating economic recession, and my personal life didn't fare much better.

In the mid-90s, Mother's health was declining. I had plenty of room in my Beverly Hills home and moved her in, providing round-the-clock nursing and in-home care. When Mother first came to live there, Odilla Gonzalez, my personal assistant for the past thirty years, was always by her side. I filled in as the night nurse until we went on the road. Then Odilla would take over. Eventually, though, I had to get 24/7 nursing care to help me and Odilla. I was used to helping organize the group's affairs, so it just came naturally that I would take on the job of managing Mother's health. I had the space and the resources to do it, so I took it on even though I didn't realize what an emotional, mental, and financial strain it would be.

Knowing that she was not doing well, I was encouraged to learn more about her past, things she didn't often talk about. I found that while attending McRae Middle School in Prescott, Arkansas, she joined a quartet that sang at various churches and camp meetings around Arkansas; and that later, during her own retirement years, as a member of God's Golden Ones at the Marin City Church of God, she and Pastor Small, Sister Lee, Sister Forman, and Uncle Jack sang for nursing homes throughout Marin County.

Her entire life, her lips never touched alcohol or tobacco. She never used a curse word, or swear word, obscene or vulgar language

of any kind, in her life. She only knew one man, intimately, romanti-
cally, sexually. Her favorite poem, "Boundless," was one that we all
loved to hear her recite.

"Boundless"

What power a woman has Mortal
man cannot rise
Above the power of a woman

They talk about a woman's sphere
As though it has a limit:
There's not a place
In earth or Heaven,

There's not a task to mankind given,
There's not a blessing or a woe,
There's not a whispered yes or no,
There's not a life or death or birth
That has a feather's weight of worth,
Without a woman in it.

Mother passed away on November 15, 2000, with me, Aaron,
Fritz, Ruth, Faun, and Jason Winters surrounding her bed at Cedars-
Sinai Medical Center in Los Angeles as she took her last breath. Jason
suggested the sisters sing "Amazing Grace" at the service, but June
said that would be too hard; so, we settled on "Zion's Hill," an old
family standard.

As with Daddy, services were held at the 23rd Avenue Church of
God in Oakland. The church was full, standing room only. Many, no
doubt, came to get a glimpse at the world-famous hometown girls,
the Pointer Sisters. We were on the program right after the choir's
musical medley of "Oh Church of God," "Leaning On The Everlasting
Arms," and "When We All Get to Heaven," songs indelible in our con-
sciousness with no need of a hymnal; there was also a duet with Uncle
Jack and Pastor Small singing, "I Will Rise Again"; and Aubrey Labrie
was there, again, reading a poem and remarks from Lizzie's dad.
Then the four of us, June, Bonnie, Ruth, and I, rose and sang mother's

favorite hymn "Zion's Hill." Every time Mother rose to preach, she would begin singing that song.

The power, passion, sincerity, and exquisite harmony with which we sang brought nearly all to tears, some to their feet, and others to shouts of joy and celebration of a life well-lived.

Her passing was difficult for me because I had been the primary caregiver for her. I assisted with bathing and grooming when I was home, and Jada always did my mother's hair since she was a licensed cosmetologist. I was used to having Mother around and making sure she was comfortable and happy. I scheduled and took her to doctor appointments, administered and recorded her consumption of medications, and paid for a housekeeper to prepare and serve her meals. Daniel P. Kunene, Fritz's father-in-law and internationally renowned poet, was compelled to compose several works to honor the tragedies that were bestowed upon the Pointer family.

For Sarah Pointer: Memories

Memories are the reality now,
Mother Sarah,
The gift you placed in
The bowls we left outside last night To receive god

You did not deny us, Mother Sarah,
Nor chide us for our presumptions
For you have now joined the ancestral spirits Who cover us like a kaross
Of well-tanned skins

You are the universal
"MOTHER"

The goddess of plenty who, but a few days ago said "I will
ride on the sunset cloud
to see how your father is doing."

Give us rain
Give us wind
Give us sun

FAIRYTALE

Give us shade
Give us light and darkness
Of day and night
Give the world
The rainbow of peace

Give us Life

Mother!

In 2003, three years after Mother passed away, my daughter Jada was diagnosed with pancreatic cancer. After a brief struggle with the disease, she passed away on June 10, 2003 at the age of 37, leaving behind her daughter Roxie. It is the most excruciating pain any parent can imagine. To be honest, there were many times that I didn't want to live myself. Why should I? What for? What kind and loving, compassionate God would do this to me? Why me? I don't hurt people, steal from people, lie to people...why me? Why take my only child? Pray to God for what? What God? What good does it do? I think if it hadn't been for my granddaughter Roxie, things would have been different. I'm not sure if I would have had the will to go on.

Anita By Daniel P. Kunene

Anita,
I heard you sing a lullaby
to let your baby sleep,
yet, you dreaded the last note, held your
breath to keep it at bay for the longest
possible moment. Tears blinded your eyes
because you feared, when she went to sleep,
you could not exchange those
mother-daughter whisperings with her anymore.

But the baby had to sleep, mother,
For the stars were beckoning impatiently
calling to her to become one of them

a star shining and dancing with them
forever in the heavens.

And you, Roxie, looked at your mother
on the verge of leaving,
you feared to bid her goodbye
and you asked mournfully,
    "Who then will guide my feet
    in this dangerous world"?
for you knew, when she left,
you could not hold on to her hand anymore.

Yet she was answering the irresistible call of the stars to be
reborn into their heavenly everlasting-ness trusting you
would see her shining among them.

Hold on to that star
it is your mother
smiling a halo on your head.

Still, the 2000s weren't done with us yet. We found out that June was a full-blown cocaine addict. We knew she had been struggling for quite some time, but we had hoped she had gotten it under control. I had decided that something more had to be done. We had to give it one more try. I felt like if we worked together as a family, we could save June from the throes of addiction. I organized an intervention involving Fritz and Aaron and my boyfriend at the time, James. We gave it our best effort, but it didn't work. In the past, Aaron had paid for overdue Hollywood motel bills and extended stay for June (and Bonnie) when they were virtually homeless, living on the streets of Hollywood. Now we needed to come up with a plan to save our baby sister.

Fritz agreed to come to L.A. from Novato, for a dangerous intervention where he had to work undercover with a wire provided by the Hollywood Police Department, CRASH Division. They wanted to corroborate certain statements by a corrupt probation officer about what was going on in June's house on Selma Avenue. Fritz got himself invited to the house by the parole officer to see for himself how well

June was doing, but things didn't turn out as planned. June's drug dealer, this guy they called "Uptown," was also the corrupt parole officer's client.

In conversation at the parole officer's home, when discussing Uptown, the drug dealer living in June's house, the parole officer told Fritz: "If Uptown leaves, another drug dealer will just come and take his place. Uptown knows drugs...how much she should take and when...that sort of thing." He couldn't believe what he was hearing. Fritz later had to come back to Hollywood to testify in court against the parole officer. It came out that she and Uptown were working together to extort money and keep June coked up.

There were a lot of things that happened to June that we had no knowledge about. We just had to love her as much as we could. June was a grown woman, and we couldn't make decisions for her. It was obvious to us that she never stopped using cocaine right up to her death. When she was diagnosed with cancer, doctors said it was all through her body. We think she knew it. She didn't want to go through the pain of chemo and radiation. Once we saw the x-rays, we knew it was just a matter of time. When she was at her sickest, she couldn't talk or swallow. Bonnie, Ruth, and I would sing to her. She would mouth, "I love you" when she had the strength. She was surrounded by love right up through the last moments of her life.

June passed away peacefully at 1:10 p.m., April 11, 2006, like a baby returning to the lap of her mother. June rested, in her final minutes of life, with me, Aaron, Fritz, and Ruth by her side. Our angel had gone to sleep with the heavenly angels. June had worked solidly for 37 years. She never had even a normal vacation: two more days in Paris or Antwerp after working there for four or five was as close as she got. Why couldn't June see and accept her own beauty, her own goodness just being June? She lived her life before she died. To honor her, Dr. Kunene was again moved to compose.

June: *A Lullaby for You*

How do I begin to speak my thoughts about you, my daughter? How do I will myself to say yes, what has been has been, And what is is? Do I confess, here, my weakness,

MOTHER

My inability to bid you farewell?
Why does the word farewell stick to my throat?

When my mind clears I find the answer I have known all along But had
forgotten, and I smile, I laugh a little as I tell myself This is not farewell, it
is an Au revoir, a Totsiens
An Auf Wiedersehn or, as we say back home in Zululand, Abakhe babo-
nana bayophinda babonane futhi
Yes, those who have once met, will meet again and again and again.

Also, remember, that in the immediate rush of grief, In my heart that was
bleeding fresh blood,
I forgot that you had got into the very core of our being
And we would thus hear forever your voice singing Jump For My Love,
I'm Ready For Love, Happiness, and so many more.
All we have to do is listen, and we will know
You have become eternally an inseparable part of us.

As for me, I will always remember that telephone call in 1994:

"Dad, it's me, June."
"June?" I say, incredulously
"Yes. We're performing at the White House. Washington DC, you know."
"We're on a short break. Dad, we're having a star dedicated to us.
Hollywood. Walk of Fame, you know."
"Oh, my goodness. Hearty congratulations."
"Dad, I'm so excited. Will you write a poem for us for the occasion?"
"Of course, of course."
I had wanted to ask you if you had met the First Dog is it overweight?
Did it eat hotdogs or something like that? But you were instantly gone.

You know, my daughter, that all of us gathered here today – your sisters,
Your brothers, your nephews, your nieces, your extended family,
Your friends of all ages and hues,
Are in awe that a star that shone so bright but a moment ago,
Has now flown beyond our ken.
So, permit us a moment to wash our emotions with tears
To come to terms with the cessation of your ability

FAIRYTALE

To speak, to laugh, to sing, to cry with us, to break bread with us
Once cleansed, we will claim you back
To dwell among us forever.

June was laid to rest at the Tamalpais Cemetery in San Rafael, California along with Dad, Mom, and Jada. Our baby sister's passing left us at a crossroads as a family and professionally. June was gone and we had to decide what to do with our group, our livelihood, the Pointer Sisters. Knowing that she had substance issues, I was always worried that something would happen. It was my job to consider the group's future and that meant taking into account all the possible risks, the most pressing being June and her fragile health, which was made worse by her frequent lapses back into heavy cocaine use.

Bonnie had left the group to go solo, and she tried to rejoin when her career slowed, but we weren't sure that she would be dedicated to the group after enjoying solo success. Now June, the spark of the group, was gone. I wasn't sure what the future looked like for us, but I was incredibly grateful that the Sterling/Winters organization stood by us during those tough times.

After such a soul-crushing decade, I wasn't even sure if there was a future for the Pointer Sisters.

Chapter 15

BONNIE 2.0

S INCE RETURNING FROM A EUROPEAN TOUR IN 2008, BONNIE, THE original Sister, the seminal artist, continued performing in venues like Pride festivals and Hard Rock Cafés around the world. Despite some of the things she's gone through, she has always worked, especially overseas where her popularity continues. After losing June, she was looking for direction just like Ruth and I were. She found it in the studio by contacting her longtime friend David Williams at Melrose Mastering. Next, she joined up with writing/producing partners Lloyd Poe and Robin Taylor and collectively they created her next album *Like a Picasso*. On that record, she sounded better than ever, and with her new partnership, the sound had a fresh, hopeful feel. It was one of her best albums and it gave her new life and new reasons to stay clean and devote herself to the music.

She had tried to record with June, but that partnership never materialized, mainly because either June was relapsing, or Bonnie was. They each battled demons. Prior to her death, June even lost her home due to the poor advice about finances and taxes. While June was unable to break the cycle, Bonnie was more successful and *Like a Picasso*, her fourth album, this time on the independent label Platinum Trini Entertainment, was proof that she had decided to embrace life.

With performers like Bonnie, throwing themselves into the creative process is often the best way to regain professional focus. Her re-emergence as a mature and enduring talent transcends any boundaries or genre: echoing the Pointer Sisters' earlier proclamation, "We can sing anything." On that album, there were fourteen rock, country, gospel, and pop tunes each performed with a level of grace and authenticity that were destined to once again land Bonnie in the spotlight.

Even though Bonnie wasn't performing with the Pointer Sisters, and hadn't for a long time, I was still happy for her success and wanted the best for her. She was always very talented and a prolific songwriter. Over the years, Bonnie had written songs for herself as well as other performers, including Marvin Gaye, Diana Ross, Smokey Robinson, and Sly Stone. She won the Tokyo Music Festival Award with "Sweet Stuff," a song that she and I wrote with Stevie Wonder. (I wasn't credited on the song "Sleeping Alone," but I wrote every word in the back of that song starting with "oh you had to go but I'm thankful for the beautiful time we had.")

Bonnie recorded "Just Cried A Tear," written by June Nelson for Monte Hellman's film *Road to Nowhere* that won the Special Lion (Career) Award at the 2010 Venice Film Festival. She also composed music for the feature film *Heavenly Bodies* for which she performed the songs "Heaven" and "The Beast in Me" for the film's soundtrack.

She is proud of her ability to continue working in this crazy business, and rightly so. She said recently, "I just got back from New York... a performance on Fire Island for Gay Pride. You damn right I'm still in the business. There was nothing like it...right? I knocked their assess out! Right? I showed up sober. It felt so good. It was in support of Gay Pride 'when the gay messiah comes, He will fall from the star of Studio 54 and appear on the sand of Fire Island's shore.'

"I had to take either a boat or seaplane to get there. It was just off of Long Island. One of the little towns was called Babylon, now ain't that a hoot? Back in, I think, '84 I did a show, at this same venue, The Pines of Fire Island, with Eartha Kitt and Grace Jones. Can you imagine...Eartha Kitt, Grace Jones, and Bonnie Pointer? Grace actually came on stage on a motorcycle. Wow, that was thirty years ago.

"After my show, they picked me up in a limo for a private party in The Hamptons. Robin S (singer of "You Got to Show Me Love") was there, and members of the Sugar Hill Gang.

"I talk with my sisters every day," Bonnie said. "I ain't mad at nobody. I used to ask about getting back in the group. How it could be so good if we could do just one more tour together. Ruthie replied, 'I'll think about it.' She'll think about it. That's not what I said when she wanted to get in the group in the first place. 'I'll think about it.'

Well, I don't ask anymore. I just call to say, 'I love you.' That's all."

In the summer of 2015, Bonnie did join us on stage at the Greek Theater in Los Angeles, performing together for the first time in over 15 years and she was set to appear on the *Discopalooza Tour* with domestic and international dates. The reason she overcame her personal demons when June didn't was because she met the right person. A man named Lonnie Jackson was the person who freed Bonnie from her freedom. They've been together ever since.

Bonnie said, "Lonnie's been really good for me. He doesn't get high; he doesn't smoke or drink—he doesn't even like coffee. He's been straight since the day he was born. He has never done drugs of any kind his whole life. Never smoked a cigarette. He was totally straight. Not even a joint. He's never done anything. That's why I liked him, because he don't do anything. He's good for me. And it was not because of religion or anything like that; it was because he had seen it around him, all his life, and seen what it did to people.

"Now, I don't do anything either. You know, it's no fun if your partner ain't doin' it with you. I do have a drink when I want to, but he doesn't do N-E-Thing! He drinks green tea and lots of water. He's been a real source of stability for me. He's got lots of friends in the neighborhood, he's been here so long. They're friends from his childhood. I really don't have friends around here: Anita is my best friend.

"I go walking in the neighborhood, almost every day. I bring treats when I go walking; when I see dogs behind a fence, I throw them a treat. I know most of the dogs' names. I don't know the owners' names, but I know the dogs. I love being outdoors, fresh air, and scenery. I love my work. I love entertaining and seeing people smile. I've never done any other kind of work. I recently had a show in Spain, in Barcelona at the Hard Rock Casino; I just got a gig in Philadelphia for December. I ain't mad at nobody. I love everybody. I'm not bitter, mad, none of that.

"I like all kinds of music, from Aretha Franklin to Janis Joplin: I don't like any genre any more than another—I like it all. If it was good, I liked it. That's my criterion: good or bad. If it's great music I liked it—from Ellington to Rhianna. I just recorded 'Merry Christmas Baby' for a new album, an Otis Redding remix. I'm hustling like a mofo. I love my work. I love show biz. 'It'll-screw-everyone-you-know' biz. 'Where-did-all-your-money-go' biz. I'm booked to do one show a month. I keep myself busy."

FAIRYTALE

Roxie, my granddaughter, even helps manage Bonnie along with other people who are on her team so I'm very happy for how her career and her personal life have turned out. In fact, she and I went to the Hollywood Museum at Hollywood and Highland, kitty corner to The Dolby Theater, on Oscar night where the 90th Academy Awards were being held. She and I were invited by Sonja Waldo to a delicious gourmet dinner, presented by Chef Paul Shoemaker of Montresor and The Glats. Each year, the dinner chairs, Lynn Briggs Neal and husband Roger Neal, honor Hollywood luminaries with a prestigious Icon Award. So that night, along with Ed Asner, the honoree was the Pointer Sisters.

Chapter 16

YE/ YOU CAN CAN

IN 2008, EVERYBODY WAS DANCING TO OUR SONG "YES WE CAN CAN" on the Internet. On YouTube, groups were performing the song in honor of Barack Obama. We reached out to everybody we could think of, including Obama's sister, to see if they would use our song. It just seemed so right. We had sung for both Bush presidents, not to mention Reagan and Clinton. I was hoping we'd get asked to sing for Obama as well, particularly because our song was being used after he said the phrase "Yes, we can."

Casting a vote for Obama was the first time I ever voted in my life. It was the first time I ever saw any point in doing so. Every other time, the election was like choosing between the devil and the deep blue sea...what's the difference? At least Obama was somebody I thought I could relate to. "Yes, We Can" was his theme, and since I always look for professional opportunities, this seemed like a slam dunk. I wish that we had gotten to perform and show him our support, especially since we had a song that fit so well with his platform, but it was not to be.

Still, I was energized by his election as president. Even though I'm an entertainer myself, Obama showed people in America and around the world that blacks could be more than entertainers and athletes in order to be successful; that the most powerful man in America, if not the world, was a black man was something to be proud of, and I was proud and shocked when he won. I've been buying Obama memorabilia everywhere I can find it. What can I say? I'm a collector at heart.

People always thought of me as reserved and content with the status quo, but Fritz had awakened my activist side early on, and just because I wasn't vocal about things as a performer, doesn't mean that I haven't always been passionate about issues that affect me, my family, and my race.

Much like Eartha Kitt had simply asked, "Why are we in Vietnam?" I would ask, why is America still in Iraq and Afghanistan, bombing people? Why was Obama, the man I had supported for president, bombing and using drones to kill people in Libya and Yemen and Syria? These are some of the poorest countries in the world; how are they a threat to the USA? Then there were all the refugees, thousands of people dying at sea. What the hell was wrong with people? Why should people even have to think about the possibility of no life on earth? This was madness! And I'm not supposed to think about this stuff and certainly not say anything about it because I'm an entertainer?

I am not *just* an entertainer. I am a human being and a citizen of the United States: A citizen of the world, with a mind of my own. I'm also a daughter, a mother, a sister, a grandmother and a taxpayer. I care, and I care deeply when I see my tax dollars, tax dollars from anybody, being wasted on stupid war, after war, after war. I am sick and tired of hearing and reading about the United States bombing another country. And why? For what? Oil? I know they were not helping people by bombing them. I often thought there should be a "tax-rebellion" until *we* can decide where our tax money was going: This time, a global tax rebellion.

Don't the people in these countries need universal tax-supported health care, college and university education, childcare and eldercare, clean water and housing and food? Hey, we need those things right here in the US. So, how were we helping the people we were at war with, this year? People in Flint, Michigan still can't drink the water. I even read the other day that the water in Oakland was just as bad. And there was what was called the "school to prison pipeline."

What had Obama and his administration done about that? Or about what Michele Alexander called *The New Jim Crow*? What had he or his administration done about the terror against black males: one every twenty-eight hours, killed by law enforcement, those sworn to protect us, somewhere in America? Mike Brown in Ferguson, Missouri, in broad daylight, and Walter Scott, in North Carolina, on camera, shot in the back while running away, while the officer responsible is found not guilty of murder, because he "felt *threatened.*" Or when Eric Garner, a black man, is choked to death by a New York City police officer, on camera, and the officer is excused, because he "*feared* for his life," as at least two other officers looked on; or, a black young man, Oscar Grant, on camera, is shot in the back while hand-cuffed on a BART platform, in Oakland; the officer was *frightened* by the handcuffed man lying face down, so pulled his hand gun, and fired, by *accident,* thinking it was his taser. These were some of the cases we know about.

Obviously, this *fear* said something about white character and psyche that needed immediate examination and hasty excision. It also said something about the value of a black president. What had it meant as far as justice for African Americans: socially, economically and politically in 2016? To quote an unintentionally profound advertisement slogan: "Where's the beef?"

I don't know what it is like in other families, but in ours we talk about these things: Aaron and Fritz, and Fritz and I, specifically; we talk about what is going on in our families, in America, and in the world. And the president is not off limits. It takes me back to sitting around the kitchen table at 1176 (18th Street) or 408 Oakland Avenue and the free, wide and uninhibited range of topics we discussed. And even today, we share book recommendations; we're always learning. Am I proud of Barak Obama? Yes, I am. Am I naïve about America and the world? No, I am not. To have world peace, we need world law.

It just drives me crazy that people think entertainers shouldn't voice their opinion because we have a larger public platform. To me, it's the exact opposite. We should share our thoughts and feelings to encourage our fans to think about things and question authority. Being an entertainer and traveling around the world, I've met all kinds of people and seen things I never thought I'd see. It opened my eyes to just how crazy the world can be and how important it is to stay aware and involved.

In 2010, Fritz told me about his and his wife's visit with David Rubinson in the picturesque hilltop town of Eze in Southern France. David was his usual hospitable and convivial self. His house was adorned with select memorabilia of Herbie Hancock, Santana, and of course The Pointer Sisters, along with his collection of classic jukeboxes and original African art. In 2009, David relocated to France to practice permaculture and sustainable, renewable food production and became a public opponent of the actions of Israel in Gaza.

Fritz and David have maintained constant communication over the past ten years. Fritz often wrote to him about the family happenings.

David,

Good to hear from you. It's complicated. I'll try to summarize as best I can. Yes, Anita has been having some health issues – both physical and emotional. They are so intertwined it's hard to separate the two. She remains depressed over Jada and June and Mother, especially Jada, her daughter and only child. So, she takes antidepressants that make, if not keep, her drowsy; and, a prescription – or combination of these – makes her nauseous.

She got too sick, or nauseous, to finish, here at Cache Creek, California, and Issa had to sing her part, when we went to see them a couple of weeks ago. Then, in Curacao, she couldn't finish the last song; did not return to the stage and was taken by ambulance to the hospital; her blood-pressure was over 200 and her blood-sugar level was too high.

When she was released from the hospital, the next morning, Ruth presented her with the cover of her book, Still So Excited. *Anita said she felt blind-sided that Ruth had kept this project pretty much a secret; that she was in and out of LA and could have and should have talked with her about it. She said she'd been working on a book about The Pointer Sisters, and Ruth presented her with a finished copy of her book, mind you, as she was leaving the hospital in Curacao. That, you might say, took her over the edge.*

She told Ruth, and told me and Aaron, that she will never work with Ruth again, because of what Anita considered Ruth's deception, dishonesty and self-ishness. To make matters worse, Anita said the title of Ruth's book, Still So Excited *is truly dishonest. Anita said she wrote "So Excited" with Trevor Lawrence. That she and Trevor were going to split the publishing 50/50. Anita said she wanted to share the publishing with Ruth and June, so she and Trevor agreed to a 40/60 split: Do the math. Anita had no idea she was going to use that title, her title.*

Ruth said that Anita had made it clear that she didn't want to have anything to do with religion and God and all that, so why talk to her? The book though not published by a Christian publishing group; the book tour is sponsored by these evangelical types; Ruth's talking about "her salvation" and Anita is not interested in any of that...and I don't blame her. Ruth said the timing was bad, but she couldn't predict that Anita would be getting sick. She had planned to tell her about the book. She said, "I wanted Anita to hear it from me before she heard about it from anywhere else. I didn't know she was going to be sick."

So, Ruth, it seemed, believed Anita thought that she didn't deserve this "achievement." Ruth, on the other hand, argued that this was her individual project: June did her own album; Anita did her own album; Bonnie did her own album, so this was her turn – her individual project.

Long story short, Anita's doctor did tell her to stop touring. She told me she was off the med-cocktails and taking just one prescribed medication; she was sounding and doing better: going out to lunch with Roxie, movies with Bonnie, swimming, walking and thinking about her next move. She was adamant about not ever working with Ruth again. Ruth, on the other hand, did not believe it was doctors' orders but Anita reacting to her book. Well, it was all that. Anita, apparently, had consented to them going on with Ruth's daughter, Issa, and granddaughter, Sadako.

Of course, thanks for your enduring and infinite concern.

Fritz

The following day, David wrote back:

Ohhhhhhhh Fritz,

I am devastated to discover Anita's situation. Thanks so much for enlightening me. I am really quite shocked, because I follow Anita on FBook, and her June P tribute page. Do you know what med(s) she was on? The blood pressure and blood sugar scares me to death. Is this supposed to be a secret? Am I not supposed to know this? What can I do to help her? What can any of us do? Let's really look at that together. It seems to me that #1 she has to be completely detoxed and cleansed of all the toxic substances she is taking. Please let's find a path we can share to help dear Anita.

Love to you both,

and many thanks for confiding in me.

DR

As far as my career in show business, I'm not sure what the future holds. I've been touring and performing for more than forty years, starting when I was just twenty years old. I've had my share of physical and mental issues which were exacerbated by the deaths of three people so important in my life—Mother, June, and my dear Jada. In 2011, I had to battle my own uterine cancer diagnosis. I had to go through surgery and chemo for six months, lost my hair and lived with the fear of death. I was despondent and taking anti-depressants that would leave me drowsy or nauseous.

Those were the conditions under which I took to the stage in Curacao that Fritz mentioned in his letter, because I was so used to performing and not stopping. My health was so fragile that I could not finish the last song, did not return to the stage, and was taken by ambulance to the hospital. Still, it's a blessing to be an original Pointer Sister, in my heart and in every way, and always will be.

I will say that surviving such devastating family losses was tough, and I think it made me strong enough to fight cancer. Konrad Leh, my manager, would meet me for every chemo treatment, holding my hand and giving me comfort. People who show that kind of concern and compassion give me the strength to keep on going. Thankfully, since December 2012, I have been completely cancer free.

Chapter 17

DANCING SAM

T THE BEGINNING OF MY STORY, I TOLD YOU ABOUT THE POINTER Sisters' exhibit called "Ever After" at the Hollywood Museum. I was able to curate that exhibit because of my penchant for collecting things. During our travels across the country and the world, I began a collection that is very close to my heart. I am a serious collector of black memorabilia. This collecting category includes any representations of black people, encompassing exoticized images of Africans made by Europeans, artifacts of African American slavery, mementos of Jim Crow-era segregation, objects associated with black celebrities, and memorabilia from the Civil Rights Movement.

The most controversial types of black memorabilia are antiques with racist caricatures, based on stereotypes that often originated in vaudeville performances. Such imagery proliferated after the Civil War to promote the myth of white supremacy in reaction to the newly freed black people. Typically, the caricatures—which could be attached to anything from toys to cookie jars to advertising tins—depict black people as happy-go-lucky buffoons and servile simpletons, such as Mammy and Uncle Tom, with oversize features like eyes and lips.

Today, I have so much black memorabilia from all over the world that it would probably fill up a basketball court. My collection includes a tin of Nigger Hair Tobacco, children's books like, *Ten Little Niggers* and *Little Black Sambo*, and an Aunt Jemima cast-iron bank, water glasses and a dinner plate from a restaurant called Coon Chicken Inn, "Mammy and Chef" wall plaques, Staffordshire figurines depicting Uncle Tom and Eve, Golliwogs from England, Blackamoor ashtrays, and even a set of slave shackles.

FAIRYTALE

I've always loved antiques, even as a little girl. My Grandma Roxie and my great-grandmother, Grandma Stevens, kept some trunks full of old clothes in the garage. Ruthie and I use to play in those old clothes, putting them on and walking around our neighborhood in West Oakland. People would laugh at us, but we didn't care. We'd be clunking down the street in old, chipped high-heeled shoes. It was funny. I just love the memories of old things, so I guess it was kind of a natural evolution for me to get into collecting. But as a child, I never saw any of the black memorabilia that I'm collecting now. Those racist caricatures were not in *our* home.

I suppose white people made these caricatures for themselves—to laugh at them, I guess. I first discovered black memorabilia in 1980. That year, I was being inducted into the *Arkansas Black Hall of Fame*, in Little Rock, Arkansas. They gave me an award for my contribution to music and had a big event for it where I met Governor Mike Huckabee. I also bought the property the old house was on. After the ceremony, we were headed to Prescott, Arkansas, where my mother's from, and we saw an antiques store. I've always loved looking around those stores, so we stopped. That's when I saw Dancing Sam, the first piece of black memorabilia that I bought. He was a painted black wooden doll, with a little string on his back and little hinges on his limbs. You hold him on top of a plywood platform, and you tap the plywood, so he jumps and dances around. Can you imagine what little white kids were being taught about black people by this "toy"?

The packaging read, "Hours and hours of fun for your children." Whoa, you mean kids would sit there and play with this for hours? Dancing Sam is black with white lips, like blackface makeup, so he intrigued me. It all started there. I began going into antiques stores and picking up black memorabilia wherever I could find it. It was amazing. It was the manifestation of what many white people used to think of black people. Some political operatives even shared that sort of sick, and sickening, images of President Obama and his gorgeous wife, Michelle. These people, clearly, are mentally ill. Racism is a mental illness.

Even today, we are repeating history. The police who were supposed to protect and serve us were killing our black youth in record numbers: it was like lynchings; the prisons were bursting at the seams with imprisoned black males. The justice system was corrupt. We were out there marching in the '60s, and racists were still killing black people today with no accountability: like it was an act of nature, like an earthquake or something that just can't be helped. The government won't take down that stupid Confederate flag. Can people fly Nazi flags in Germany? No. It's against the law. And since we were here doing all that labor for 400 years for no pay, why don't we get a tax break? Why do the corporations get a tax break? Why don't Facebook and Amazon have to pay taxes?

I'm sometimes so disappointed, disgusted really, with some of the aspects of our country, especially the economic system and the racism. Maybe that's why I collect these racist images, because I want to get them off the market. But also, they remind me of who I am compared to what some may think of me and my race, and I prove them wrong every day of my being. We're not buffoons; we're not stupid, and we're not just dancing and singing *all the time.* Even though that's what I do for a living, I'm certainly a lot more than that—a mother, grandmother, sister, aunt, songwriter, investor, property owner, and friend.

Speaking of friends, I started accumulating vinyl albums when I bought my friend and former assistant Gina Gladstock's vast record collection, which had everything from Jimi Hendrix to Madonna. And I have all The Pointer Sisters', our albums, the vinyl LPs and the 45s. It was a history lesson to listen to records by Fats Waller, Ella Fitzgerald, and Sarah Vaughan: all these old artists that went before me and paved the way. I don't take them lightly. They really made a difference in my life. That was why I kept a lot of these old things. This is also "memorabilia," and it reminds me of how I started off learning about music.

My black albums and memorabilia collection encompass all representations of black people, from negative to positive. I wish I had focused on one type of thing, but I just bought every piece of black memorabilia I found. There wasn't a whole lot of it still out there when I started collecting. I don't know who got it all—maybe Whoopi Goldberg? I found paper—stuff like postcards and advertisements. I have a list of slave auctions. I have ceramics and wooden objects. I have potholders, cookie jars, banks, toys, dolls, aprons, hair combs, and hair grease tins. I collected Michael Jackson memorabilia, Michael Jordan memorabilia, Muhammad Ali memorabilia, Louis Armstrong

FAIRYTALE

"Satchmo" memorabilia, and dolls of Flip Wilson. I just collected anything that I saw that was related to the black experience; and also some Native American objects like Kachina dolls. I knew from way back that my roots are deep...really, that was the reason I went to Egypt. I knew that Black History, my history, did not begin on a plantation or in a jungle.

We were here, on this planet earth, and here in America from its beginning. Our Grandma Stevens was a full-blooded Cherokee Indian whose daughter (Grandma Roxie) married an African man (Granddaddy Fritz).

My collection is filled with a lot of racist caricatures. I donated an image from a *Cream of Wheat* advertising campaign to the Civil Rights Institute in Birmingham, Alabama. It showed a black man pulling a cart like a mule with a little white boy driving the cart with a whip. It was just despicable. But it reminded me that everybody did not love you and that you had to love yourself. You were not a buffoon. Many artists tried to depict black people in insulting ways, but I thought big lips and big booties were beautiful. Some of the caricatures looked beautiful to me, even if they were meant to be jokes. Today, many white starlets are trying to get that look filling their lips with injections. We had always had that. And getting fake booties, are you kidding me? We've always had that, too. Imitation is the highest form of flattery, right?

These items are a history lesson. When the Civil War ended, white people did not want to praise or congratulate black people. They wanted white people to continue to think that black people were stupid and couldn't do anything but sing and dance, take care of *their* kids, and work for them for free. That is the disgusting part. People today have to search their hearts to see if they have any evil feelings toward another people, another race.

I think it's important for people to be aware of these memorabilia items, of this history. My granddaughter, Roxie, never knew about any of this stuff. She was never confronted with a "Whites on one side and Coloreds on the other side" sign. It is important to know history; if you don't know it, you're doomed to repeat it. I don't ever want people to think this way about my people ever again, because it's just not so.

We are a beautiful people, and we are not going around getting

DANCING SAM

kicked in the head by mules like the cast-iron banks depict. It may seem like it's getting better, but when I saw the news about the mass murder at the AME church in Charleston, South Carolina—holy shit! How would you know that someone is going to be that evil in this day? I just can't believe that young white man, who went to that church, prayed with and then shot those nine people. It was a sick and depraved terrorist attack.

And the media says, "he's crazy." The media. Not doctors, not psychiatrists, not psychologists, but the TV news. What if he had been a Muslim and went into a church and killed nine white Americans? Would he just be called "crazy?" No. He would be considered a terrorist. And he is a terrorist: a white radical Christian terrorist. The same tradition of Christian terrorism that was responsible for Native American genocide, African slavery and colonialism, Hiroshima and Nagisaki, and the Jewish Holocaust, for that matter.

The government should investigate his family, his school, his church, his pastor, his friends, the websites he looked at, to find out who taught him to hate like this. Obviously, being a ninth-grade dropout, all he had going for him was being white. Then I read that after the police arrested him, they actually took him for a hamburger at Burger King. Too many of these white people in America believe that they deserve to be respected and treated better than black people, even when a white Christian terrorist just murdered nine of their fellow citizens: not enemies, their fellow citizens! ... Nine fellow human beings, for Christ's sake!

It hurts my heart to see that we're going through this shit when we fought so hard in the '60s to make people appreciate that we are human, and we do matter. Racists, especially the police and justice system, still do things that destroy black people's lives, and it makes me cry. It hurts me to see that there are so many evil people in this world, still. Why can't we grow up and treat other people like we want to be treated?

Do I believe in the death penalty? No. Would you want to be treated that way? No. I think the death penalty is a disgrace to our society. If it's supposed to be an example, then why isn't it shown in newspapers and on television news and everybody invited to watch it? Either do this or shut up about killing someone as an example. The death penalty is premeditated murder. It's about revenge and

157

retaliation; I'm about compassion and justice, even reparations and, of course, love.

No, this killer should not be free and walking the streets. But Daddy use to say in one of his sermons, "There is none righteous, no, not one." So, I can't throw the first stone or be part of the firing squad, or lethal injection, and help and watch somebody die. Then, all this poppycock from the Supreme Court, no less, about "the real judgement is not pronounced in this world, but in the next." So, it's okay to kill someone if you believe there is a heaven.

I am grateful for the #BlackLivesMatter campaign. For hundreds of years, white supremacists would kill our people with no repercussions. Even my grandmother, my father's mother, was killed in Little Rock when she was trying to catch a street car. The driver just took off and knocked her backward. She hit her head on the cement pavement. Nobody did anything to help her. She died there. And that was the least of things that have happened to black people in the South and all over America. And there are Americans who want to spread *this system* globally.

I remember my mother's mother telling me how the people in Prescott, Arkansas paid my uncle a nickel to get into a monkey cage, when the circus was in town. She got so mad, yelling, "You get out of there! Don't you let them do that to you!" It's horrible the way some white people can think they are better than others just because they have white skin. Such people "need a nigger" and if they don't have one, they'll try to create one. I wasn't raised that way. "I am not your nigger" as James Baldwin said. James Baldwin was Fritz's all-time favorite writer. He has read, and has autographed copies of, all Baldwin's books: *Go Tell It on the Mountain, Another Country, The Fire Next Time, If Beale Could Talk, Blues For Mr. Charlie*... It was certainly *the* highlight of his life when Baldwin came to Decorah, Iowa and Luther College to lecture, and Fritz was able to spend the day with him.

Baldwin spoke, in the Luther College Chapel, about "infantile US foreign policy" predicated on the proverbial myth "The Enemy Is at The Gate." So, nothing can be done about health care for all, or crumbling school systems and infrastructure, childcare and eldercare, and tax-supported technical college and university education: because "The enemy is at the gate. The Russian Bogeyman is coming to get us."

DANCING SAM

A lot of the people supporting Forty-Five, America's president—he will never be my president—were hallucinating that they, too, may someday have $50 billion in the bank, enjoy celebrity status, and live a lavish lifestyle: "He's gonna make us all millionaires," said one completely lost soul. In fact, there's something sick about a system that allowed one person to have that much money: especially with all the homelessness and the poverty I see right here in L.A.

For the second time in my life, I voted: I voted for Hillary Clinton. I don't always agree with her either. We were back to "the devil and the deep blue sea." I really liked what Jill Stein had to say and Bernie Sanders, so it was one of those "hold your nose" and vote for the least evil one. I don't like how she promoted the bombing of Libya and murdered Gaddafi. I liked some of the things Gaddafi was doing and wanted to do for Africa: one currency for the continent of Africa. Why not? Education, healthcare, and childcare to the age of five, paid for by taxes and money from their oil.

Forty-five was an example of how being dumb and stupid became a good thing in America. Can you imagine...ignorance a virtue? Forty-five was proud of being ignorant about people and the world. It was clear he didn't read books and probably couldn't write more than a couple of sentences at a time. He was also a racist and white supremacist. Look at the people he appointed to his cabinet: one guy, an outspoken supporter of the KKK, some radio host guy. He hired people to protect the environment who don't believe the environment needed protecting or that global warming was real. This dangerous dimwit believed it was a hoax started by China. He hired this woman to oversee public education, a billionaire, who didn't believe in public education. Now, this was a biggy: Forty-Five's dumb thinking on nuclear and environmental issues threatened the survival of human beings and life on this planet. Now, that was serious.

What, I shouldn't know or care about these things because I'm an *entertainer*?

DI/COGRAPHY

The Pointer Sisters
(Bonnie Pointer, June Pointer, Anita Pointer, and Ruth Pointer)

The Pointer Sisters - 1973
"Yes We Can Can"
"Cloudburst"
"Jada"
"River Boulevard"
"Old Songs"
"That's How I Feel"
"Sugar"
"Pains and Tears"
"Wang Dang Doodle"

That's A Plenty – 1974
"Bangin' on the Pipes"/"Steam Heat" (medley)
"Salt Peanuts"
"Grinning in Your Face"
"Shaky Flat Blues"
"That's a Plenty"/"Surfeit, U.S.A." (medley)
"Little Pony"
"Fairytale"
"Black Coffee"
"Love In Them There Hills"

Live at the Opera House – 1974
"Overture – Prelude to Islandia"
"Walk-On"
"Salt Peanuts"
"Shaky Flat Blues"
"Fairytale"
"Cloudburst"
"Jada"
"Black Coffee"
"Let It Be Me"
"Hands Up"/"Wang Dang Doodle" (medley)

DIƧCOGRAPHY

"Old Songs"/"That's a Plenty"/"Bei Mir Bist Du Schoen" (medley)
"Steam Heat"
"Yes We Can Can"
"Love In Them There Hills"
"Walk-Off"

Steppin' – 1975
"How Long (Betcha' Got a Check on the Side)"
"Sleeping Alone"
"Easy Days"
"Chainey Do"
"I Ain't Got Nothin' But the Blues" (medley)
"Save the Bones for Henry Jones"
"Wanting Things"
"Going Down Slowly"

The Best of The Pointer Sisters – 1976
"You Gotta Believe"
"Black Coffee"
"Wang Dang Doodle"
"Salt Peanuts"
"Steam Heat"
"Cloudburst"
"Easy Days"
"Jada"
"That's a Plenty"/"Surfeit, U.S.A." (medley)
"Little Pony"
"Sugar"
"Yes We Can Can"
"Sleeping Alone"
"Fairytale"
"Shaky Flat Blues"
"Going Down Slowly"
"How Long"

Having A Party – 1977
"Having a Party"
"Don't It Drive You Crazy"

"I Need a Man"
"Waiting on You"
"I'll Get by Without You"
"Bring Your Sweet Stuff Home to Me"
"Lonely Gal"

Pointer Sisters (Anita Pointer, June Pointer and Ruth Pointer)
Energy – 1978
"Lay It on the Line"
"Dirty Work"
"Hypnotized"
"As I Come of Age"
"Come and Get Your Love"
"Happiness"
"Fire"
"Angry Eyes"
"Echoes of Love"
"Everybody Is a Star"

Priority – 1979
"Who Do You Love"
"All Your Love"
"Dreaming as One"
"Turned Up Too Late"
"Happy"
"Blind Faith"
"Don't Let a Thief Steal into Your Heart"
"(She Got) The Fever"
"The Shape I'm In"

Special Things – 1980
"Could I Be Dreaming"
"He's So Shy"
"The Love Too Good to Last"
"Evil"
"Save This Night for Love"
"We've Got the Power"

DI/COGRAPHY

"Where Did the Time Go"
"Special Things"
"Here Is Where Your Love Belongs"

Black & White – 1981
"Sweet Lover Man"
"Someday We'll Be Together"
"Take My Heart, Take My Soul"
"Slow Hand"
"We're Gonna Make It"
"What a Surprise"
"Got to Find Love"
"Fall in Love Again"
"Should I Do It"

So Excited! – 1982
"I'm So Excited"
"See How the Love Goes"
"All of You"
"Heart Beat"
"If You Wanna Get Back Your Lady"
"I Feel for You"
"Heart to Heart"
"American Music"

Break Out – 1983
"Jump (For My Love)"
"Automatic"
"Baby, Come and Get It"
"I Need You"
"Dance Electric"
"Neutron Dance"
"Easy Persuasion"
"Nightline"
"Telegraph Your Love"
"Operator"

FAIRYTALE

Break Out – 1984 (re-release)
"Jump (For My Love)"
"Automatic"
"I'm So Excited"
"I Need You"
"Neutron Dance"
"Dance Electric"
"Easy Persuasion"
"Baby, Come and Get It"
"Telegraph Your Love"
"Operator"

Contact – 1985
"Twist My Arm"
"Hey You"
"Pound, Pound, Pound"
"Back in My Arms"
"Burn Down the Night"
"Bodies and Souls"
"Dare Me"
"Freedom"

Hot Together – 1986
"My Life"
"Mercury Rising"
"Goldmine"
"All I Know Is the Way I Feel"
"Say the Word"
"Hot Together"
"Sexual Power"
"Set Me Free"
"Taste"
"Eyes Don't Lie"

Serious Slammin' – 1988
"Serious Slammin'"
"Shut Up and Dance"
"Moonlight Dancing"

DIƧCOGRAPHY

"He Turned Me Out"
"Flirtatious"
"My Life" (remix)
"I'm in Love"
"Pride"
"Uh-Uh"
"I Will Be There"

Right Rhythm – 1990
"Friends' Advice (Don't Take It)"
"Man With the Right Rhythm"
"Real Life"
"After You"
"You Knocked the Love (Right Outta My Heart)"
"Billy Said Yes"
"Insanity"
"What a Woman Wants"
"Where Have You Been?"
"(We Just Wanna) Thank You"

Only Sisters Can Do That – 1993
"It Ain't a Man's World"
"I Want Fireworks"
"Don't Walk Away"
"Eyes Like a Child"
"Only Sisters Can Do That"
"Feel for the Physical"
"Tell It to My Heart"
"Vibe Time"
"Lose Myself to Find Myself"
"Sex, Love or Money"

Highlights from Ain't Misbehavin' - 1996
Act I
"Ain't Misbehavin'"
"Lookin' Good but Feelin' Bad"
"'T Ain't Nobody's Bizness"
"Honeysuckle Rose"

FAIRYTALE

"Squeeze Me"
"Handful of Keys"
"I've Got a Feeling I'm Falling"
"How Ya Baby"
"Jitterbug Waltz"
"Ladies Who Sing with the Band"
"Yacht Club Swing"
"When the Nylons Bloom Again"
"Cash for Your Trash"
"Off-Time"
"The Joint is Jumpin'"
Act II
"Spreadin' Rhythm Around"
"Lounging at the Waldorf"
"The Viper's Drag"
"Mean to Me"
"Your Feet's Too Big"
"That Ain't Right"
"Keepin' Out of Mischief Now"
"Find Out What They Like"
"Fat and Greasy"
"Black and Blue"
"I'm Gonna Sit Right Down and Write Myself a Letter"
"Two Sleepy People"
"I've Got my Fingers Crossed"
"I Can't Give You Anything but Love"
"It's a Sin to Tell a Lie"
"Honeysuckle Band"

The Pointer Sisters: Live in Billings – 2004
Including "Fairytale," "Chain of Fools," "Yes We Can Can," "I'm
So Excited!"

The Pointer Sisters Favorites – 2008
Including "I'm So Excited," "Happiness," "He's So Shy," "Auto-
matic," "Yes We Can Can," "Dare Me," "Slow Hand," "Fire,"
"Neutron Dance," "Jump (For My Love)"

DISCOGRAPHY

Bonnie Pointer

Bonnie Pointer (Red Album), Motown, 1978

Bonnie Pointer (Purple Album), Motown, 1979

If the Price Is Right, Private I Records, 1984

Like A Picasso, Platinum Trini Records, 2011

June Pointer

Baby Sister, Planet Records, 1983

June Pointer, Columbia Records, 1989

Anita Pointer

Love for What It Is, RCA, 1987

TV/Movie Appearances (partial list)

1973	*The Helen Reddy Show*
	Flip
	One More Time (TV Special)
	Soul Train
	The Tonight Show
1974	*Gala du Midem*
	Russell Harty Plus
	In Concert
	Dinah!
	The Bob Braun Show
	The Hollywood Palladium
	The Sound of Petula
	Soundstage
	The Mike Douglas Show
	The Carol Burnett Show
1975	*Cher*
1976	*Super Night at the Super Bowl*
	The Captain and Tennille
	Andy
	Car Wash (movie)
1977	*The Merv Griffin Show*
	American Bandstand
	Sesame Street
1979	*Hollywood's Greatest Wrap Party*
	Numbero Un
	Top of the Pops
1980	*The Captain and Tennille Show*
	The Midnight Special
	Marie
1981	*Solid Gold*
	The Love Boat

TV/MOVIE APPEARANCES

1982   *Macy's Thanksgiving Day Parade*

1983   *Suzanne Somers...And 10,000 G.I.s*
        Leather and Lace
        Gimme a Break!

1985   *We Are the World: The Story Behind the Song*
        The 12th Annual American Music Awards
        Champs-Elysees

1988   *20th NAACP Image Awards*
        Jerry Lewis MDA Labor Day Telethon

1989   *Live! With Kelly*

1990   *Into the Night*
        Big Break

1991   *Bob Hope's Christmas Cheer from Saudi Arabia*
        The 18th Annual American Music Awards

1993   *Maury*

1994   *Vicki!*

1995   *We Are the World: A 10th Anniversary Tribute*

1996   *The Tonight Show with Jay Leno*

1998   *Macy's Thanksgiving Day Parade*

2001   *A Capitol Fourth*

2003   *The Disco Ball*

2004   *Pointer Sisters: Live in Montana 2004*

2006   *Podium*

2012   *TV One Night Only: Live from the Essence Music Festival*

2013   *Night of the Proms*

POINTER FAMILY HISTORY

Paul Pointer, born 1830 in North Carolina, is the earliest known Pointer. His wife, **Matilda Pointer** was born 1840 in Mississippi. We don't know the cities. These were our great-great grandparents. Fritz and I were certainly proud and pleased to know that Paul, from 1861-1865, was a member of the 3rd United States Colored Heavy Artillery. We abhor war but what, in this case, does one do? His parents were unknown. After the Civil War, Paul took up residence in Memphis, Tennessee where he was a laborer and Matilda was a housekeeper. Matilda was 10 years younger than Paul but died at a relatively young age; he had remarried at the age of 38 to a lady by the name of **Ida Lock**.

Abraham (Griffin) Pointer, our paternal great-grandfather, was born in 1849 in Richmond, Virginia. Harry and Sara Griffin were the parents of Abraham Griffin. Extant records reveal they were African people who were owned by the Griffin Plantation in Richmond, Virginia. Harry and Sara had five children in addition to **Abraham**. The Griffin Plantation owners sold three of the children to the Pointer Plantation, also in Richmond, Virginia. Harry Jr. and the two daughters remained on the Griffin Plantation while Henry, Joe, and **Abraham** were torn away from their parents.

With the new plantation came a new slave name – Pointer. Abraham (Griffin) Pointer, after the Emancipation Proclamation in 1865, moved to Memphis, Tennessee. While living in Memphis, he met a young woman named **Chanie Marriah Harding**. Chanie was living in Memphis with her mother, Mary Harding, (born in Lucy, Tennessee) her father (name unknown), her sister Florida, and her three brothers Edom, Simon, and Daniel. In 1870, Abraham and Chanie married in Memphis. Together they had fourteen children.

What we learn from (Aunt) Eva Pointer's entries in "Herman Pointer's Book" (his *Bible*) is that **Herman Pointer**, our paternal grandfather, was born on October 6, 1875 in Memphis, Tennessee, and had thirteen (13) brothers and sisters: Junja Pointer (June 11, 1872), Ernest Pointer (January 10, 1874), **Herman Pointer (October 6, 1875)**, Addie Pointer (January 12, 1878), Bertha Pointer (June 9, 1880), Charlotte

Pointer (April 26, 1882), Temothy (a daughter) Pointer (December 7, 1884), Effie Pointer (January12, 1887), Ellis Pointer (July 21, 1888), Bernice Pointer (December 20, 1890), Philander Pointer (February 13, 1894), Luke Elton Pointer (January 21, 1895), Ira Abraham Pointer (March 11, 1897) and finally, Roosevelt Pointer (September 6, 1900).

Abraham and Chanie then moved to the state of Arkansas. They farmed the land just as they had in Tennessee. Only four of the children moved to Arkansas, initially. Those children were **Herman**, Temothy (a sister), Ira Abraham, and Ellis Windbush. Born in Memphis, Tennessee in 1857, Chanie was 92 years old when she died.

The 1920 United States Federal Census also put our grandfather's, Herman's, birth year in 1875, again, somewhere in Tennessee. At the time of this census (1920) **Herman** was listed as 44 years of age and home was Little Rock Ward 1, Pulaski, Arkansas. His race was listed as Mulatto in the 1880 census and Black in the 1920 census. His wife, **Frankie Pointer**, our paternal grandmother, was listed as 48 at the time of this census. Their children were **Eva (Kennedy) Pointer** (20), **Elton "Daddy" Pointer** (19).

We don't know very much at all about Aunt Eva. In addition to Papa's *Bible*, which she passed down to us, we have an original, framed, copy of her Diploma from Philander Smith College, Normal Department, in Little Rock, Arkansas dated the twenty ninth of May 1919. It is one of our favorite family heirlooms and mentions her "proficiency in scholarship," and "integrity of character." There were lessons in this. At some point, she lived in Chicago because we would receive Birthday and Christmas cards from her with a dollar inside. Talk about happy!

Our maternal great-grandparents: **Cyrus Silas** (1860), and his wife, **Catherine Silas** (1862) according to the 1910 U.S. Census, were both born in Texas, no city noted. Uncle Leon (Silas) told us later that Cyrus and his wife, Catherine, came to Arkansas in 1899 from **Atlanta, Texas.**

According to Uncle Leon, a Mr. Will Bemis came to Atlanta recruiting men to rebuild the Bemis (lumber) Mills, in Roseboro, Arkansas, which had burned down. Cyrus Silas was one of his first recruits. He also told us that Cyrus' father, Horace (Hopkins) Silas, chose the name *Silas* from *The Bible*: from the *Book of Acts* 16:25 – 31 where Apostle Paul takes Silas as his companion and they traveled through Syria.

They were arrested, flogged, and imprisoned for "causing a public nuisance"—for spreading the message of peace: sort of like Jesus, and Gandhi, and Martin Luther King. "Paul and Silas in Jail" is also a gospel blues song written by Washington Phillips (1880-1954) and recorded by him, in 1927. It was also a rather precise metaphor for the mass-incarceration of Black men in America, then and now (2020).

Thankfully, a name with meaning that was beyond the plantation. Horace Silas refused to take the *slave-master's* name and, instead, chose a name from *The Bible* – Silas. "Silas" was, perhaps, a little less *offensive* than, say, Kunta Kinte.

Fritz Silas (1889-1967) our maternal grandfather was one of eight children of Cyrus and Catie: four daughters, Hattie (1892), Gustava (1895), Addie (n.d.), Elizabeth (n.d.), and four sons: John Henry (1897), Dee (1899), Horace (1903) and, of course, the man we called **"Grand-daddy Fritz."** Only Dee and Horace were born in Arkansas, Fritz, and the other three children were born in Texas.

Mother's dad, Granddaddy Fritz, was born in 1889 in Marshall, Texas and worked at Bemis' Sawmill as a lumber grader. Mother told me he was not paid the same as the white graders. He even trained some who were promoted over him. When they bought their house on Green Lawn Street, the mortgage payments were $5.25 per month. After several years of making payments, the Housing Authority in Memphis, Tennessee claimed that no payments had been made all those years. Fortunately, Granddaddy had saved all of his receipts. I learned from that.

To make ends meet, Granddaddy Fritz and his sixteen-year old son, Leon, drove a horse and buggy around Prescott selling ice from a wagon in summer, and wood in the winter. He also opened a restaurant next to the five-bedroom, corner-lot house at 201 Green Lawn Street that Mother grew up in and where I stayed when I visited. It was Uncle Leon who told us: Neighboring blacks use to say Prescott blacks were spoiled. We lived all over Prescott. We had a rough time and got teased by blacks from Hope and Guerdon and all around. There was, they thought, no black *section* in Prescott; still, Gramma would go to the back door of white neighbors across the street. When Granddaddy Fritz died in 1967, in Oakland, we took his body back to Prescott, Arkansas.

Roxie Stevens (Silas) was born May 12, 1892, in Arkadelphia,

Arkansas, "**Grandma Roxie's**" parents, our great-grandparents, were **Adam** and **Sarah Stevens**. The most remembered story about Adam was that he was totally illiterate until "called" to the ministry, at which time he learned to read *The Bible*, and "only" *The Bible*. As family oral tradition had it, if given a book or newspaper he could not read it, only *The Bible*. We, unfortunately, never met Grandpa Adam, never in the flesh. We understood he was a preacher and a Mason, a Prince Hall Mason.

We did meet, ever so briefly, **Grandma Stevens** when she came to live with us in Oakland during the fifties. She was 100 years old then and died when she was 102. She dipped snuff and used a spittoon quite accurately. She was decidedly Indian, Cherokee we think, color, cheekbones, the long braid she wore that we, eventually, kept in her framed picture. She died in the downstairs flat of our home at 1176 18th Street, Oakland. We Pointers and Silases, elders and children, were around her bed when she took her last, very deep, breath. If death could be beautiful this was.

Grandma Roxie, her daughter, also came from a large family including three sisters: Cora, Daisy and Lucille, and four brothers: Tom, John, Moody and Luke. From Arkadelphia the Stevens moved to Prescott, Arkansas where Roxie the little girl became Roxie the young woman. It was in Prescott that she met and later married **Fritz Silas**, on June 29, 1911. Reverend A.W. Harthorn performed the marriage.

A spiritual woman, a religiously inclined woman, a woman of tremendous faith, **Grandma Roxie**, as we said, "cast her lot" with the Church of God in Prescott, Arkansas in September 1921 under the ministry of Reverend A.L. Auston of Gurdon, Arkansas. She helped in the early years of the Church of God in Prescott: she sang in the choir, taught Sunday school, and tithed. Grandma Roxie would often recite, clearly and with conviction, her favorite Biblical verses like: "Love suffers long," and then ask provocatively, "How long is long?" or lyrics of a hymn like, "It is well with my soul"; or poem like, "A Woman's Worth," in a testimony before an entire congregation or in prayer meetings of five to ten in our house on 18th St. When she passed in 1987, she had fourteen grandchildren (we represented six), sixteen great-grandchildren, and seven great-great grandchildren.

Fritz and Roxie Silas had six children: Fritz Jr. (1913), Leon Hunter (November 18, 1919), Theron "Jack," (1928), Thomas (n.d.), Azie (n.d.), and, of course, our mother, **Sarah Elizabeth Silas** (January 13, 1924).

Family oral tradition, our mother, told us that Fritz Jr. died because he wouldn't miss work. He was sick. He should have stayed home. He insisted. His sickness, pneumonia, got worse, and he passed. He was 24. There was an obvious lesson here and Sarah, our mother, passed that name on to her second son.

The second of the six Silases, Leon Hunter, attended McRae School in Prescott, Arkansas. In 1938, he married Clara Mae Smith. They had a trio of boys: William Harold (we called him "Pie"), Leon Jr., and Paul Theron.

Uncle Leon, as we called him, was an industrious, philosophical visionary. If you asked him, he would probably tell you that he invented the word *entrepreneur*. While a teenager in Prescott, Arkansas, he had two businesses: in the summer, selling ice in the morning and, in the afternoon, newspapers, door-to-door, to the small businesses in the small downtown; and, in the winter, firewood.

Once, so we were told by our mother, our family Griotte, that her brother, Uncle Leon, to pick-up a little extra change, was lured by a circus come to town, and ended up in a cage and paraded through town. He cried. Our grandparents were, of course, furious and we thought there was a lesson in that: something about letting go of something that may ensnare, entrap you. Granddaddy Fritz told a story his father told him of how his people in Africa would catch monkeys: a simple, benign trap with a banana in it. The monkey could put his hand in and grab the banana but was too stupid to let it go to get away, and would hold it, squirming until someone came and took him or her away.

As a young man, Uncle Leon opened a little neighborhood restaurant; he told us that his lack of success was due to the fact that his father, our Granddaddy Fritz, wouldn't allow him to put a jukebox in the place, so he settled for a radio. Uncle Leon left Arkansas on a venture that took him to New York City, Chicago, and later Los Angeles. He spent two years in military service, improved his cooking skills, moved to Oakland in 1953, and opened a couple of restaurants on East 14th Street. For a while, Mother and Aunt Della and Aunt Clara Mae worked with him. He was a dominant talker at family gatherings. One of his favorite expressions was, "I talk a lot because I got a lot to talk about."

PHOTO COLLECTION

FAIRYTALE

01. Our Great Grandparents, Paul Pointer (born 1830).

02. Matilda Pointer (born 1840).

03. Herman "Papa" Pointer (born 1875) circa 1920s.

04. Frankie Pointer (born 1882) circa 1930s.
Collection of the Authors.

05. Elton Pointer, probably Arkansas, circa 1930s.
Collection of the Authors.

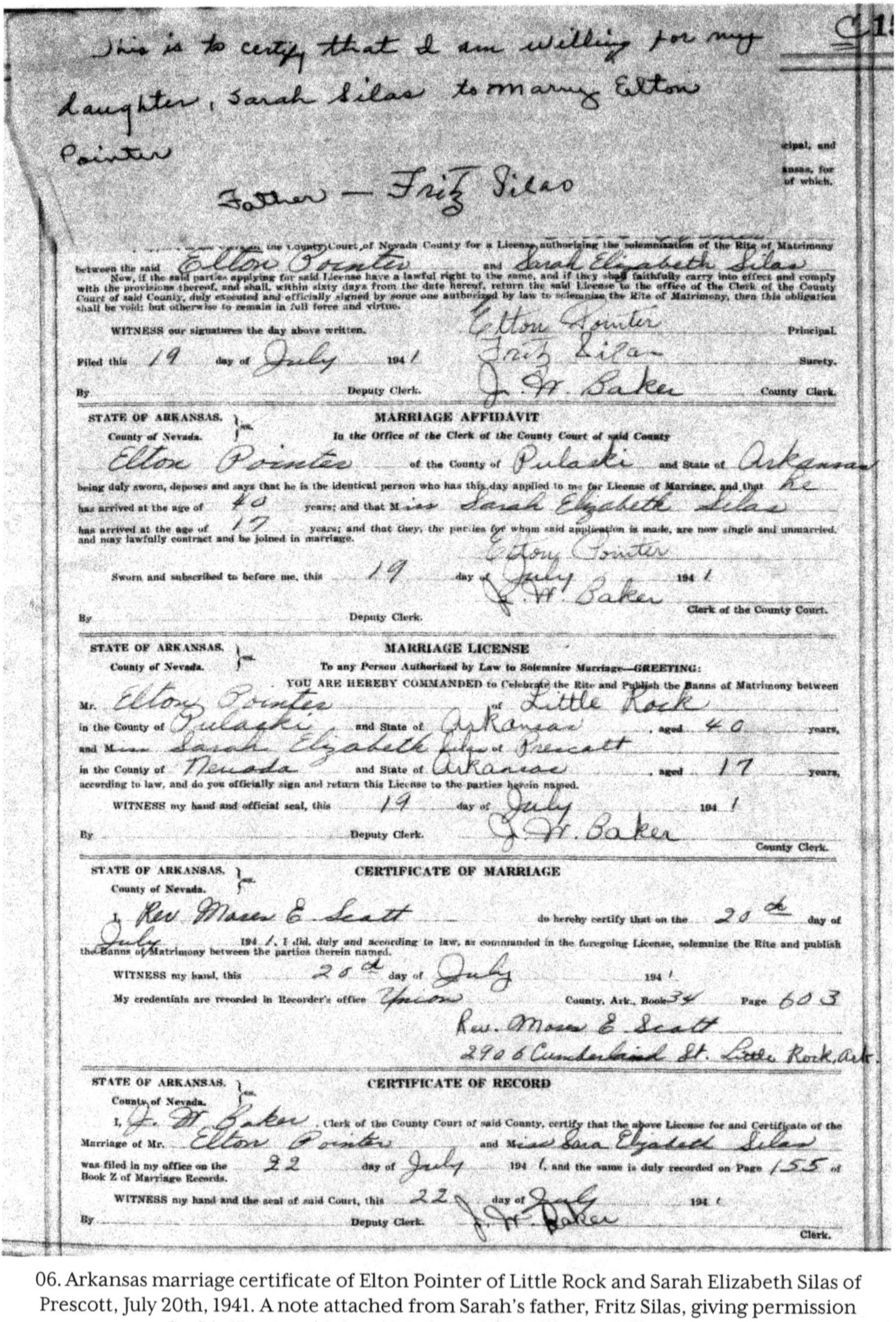

This is to certify that I am willing for my daughter, Sarah Silas to marry Elton Pointer

Father — Fritz Silas

...cipal, and ...ansas, for ... of which,

... the County Court of Nevada County for a License authorizing the solemnization of the Rite of Matrimony between the said Elton Pointer and Sarah Elizabeth Silas

Now, if the said parties applying for said License have a lawful right to the same, and if they shall faithfully carry into effect and comply with the provisions thereof, and shall, within sixty days from the date hereof, return the said License to the office of the Clerk of the County Court of said County, duly executed and officially signed by some one authorized by law to solemnize the Rite of Matrimony, then this obligation shall be void; but otherwise to remain in full force and virtue.

WITNESS our signatures the day above written. Elton Pointer Principal.

Filed this 19 day of July 1941 Fritz Silas Surety.

By Deputy Clerk. J. W. Baker County Clerk.

STATE OF ARKANSAS, County of Nevada.

MARRIAGE AFFIDAVIT

In the Office of the Clerk of the County Court of said County

Elton Pointer of the County of Pulaski and State of Arkansas being duly sworn, deposes and says that he is the identical person who has this day applied to me for License of Marriage, and that he has arrived at the age of 40 years; and that Miss Sarah Elizabeth Silas has arrived at the age of 17 years; and that they, the parties for whom said application is made, are now single and unmarried, and may lawfully contract and be joined in marriage.

Elton Pointer

Sworn and subscribed to before me, this 19 day of July 1941

By Deputy Clerk. J. W. Baker Clerk of the County Court.

STATE OF ARKANSAS, County of Nevada.

MARRIAGE LICENSE

To any Person Authorized by Law to Solemnize Marriage—GREETING:

YOU ARE HEREBY COMMANDED to Celebrate the Rite and Publish the Banns of Matrimony between Mr. Elton Pointer of Little Rock in the County of Pulaski and State of Arkansas, aged 40 years, and Miss Sarah Elizabeth Silas of Prescott in the County of Nevada and State of Arkansas, aged 17 years, according to law, and do you officially sign and return this License to the parties herein named.

WITNESS my hand and official seal, this 19 day of July 1941

By Deputy Clerk. J. W. Baker County Clerk.

STATE OF ARKANSAS, County of Nevada.

CERTIFICATE OF MARRIAGE

I, Rev. Moses E. Scott do hereby certify that on the 20th day of July 1941, I did, duly and according to law, as commanded in the foregoing License, solemnize the Rite and publish the Banns of Matrimony between the parties therein named.

WITNESS my hand, this 20th day of July 1941

My credentials are recorded in Recorder's office Union County, Ark., Book 34 Page 603

Rev. Moses E. Scott
2906 Cumberland St. Little Rock, Ark.

STATE OF ARKANSAS, County of Nevada.

CERTIFICATE OF RECORD

I, J. W. Baker, Clerk of the County Court of said County, certify that the above License for and Certificate of the Marriage of Mr. Elton Pointer and Miss Sara Elizabeth Silas was filed in my office on the 22 day of July 1941, and the same is duly recorded on Page 155 of Book Z of Marriage Records.

WITNESS my hand and the seal of said Court, this 22 day of July 1941

By Deputy Clerk. J. W. Baker Clerk.

06. Arkansas marriage certificate of Elton Pointer of Little Rock and Sarah Elizabeth Silas of Prescott, July 20th, 1941. A note attached from Sarah's father, Fritz Silas, giving permission for his 17-year-old daughter to wed the 40-year-old Preacher.

07. Sarah and Elton with Aaron and Fritz Pointer, 1945.
Collection of the Authors.

08. The only known photograph of the West Oakland Church
of God, circa 1950s. Collection of the Authors.

09. Pointer and Silas families at 1176 18th Street Oakland, CA. (LtoR top row) Herman Pointer, Fritz and Roxie Silas, Aunts Della, Wilama, and Clara Silas, Sarah and Elton Pointer, Imogene Lee. (LtoR bottom row) Theron "Jack", J.W Silas, Leon Silas, unknown identities of the 3 young boys in photo. Collection of the Authors.

10. Fritz (far left,) Aaron (far right,) and cousin Paul Silas (third row back, "head popping up,") at DeFremery Recreation Center. Photo by E.F. Josephs / Courtesy Careth Reid.

11. Anita as toddler in DeFremery Park.

12. (LtoR) Ruth, Bonnie and Anita holding hands.

13. (LtoR) Anita, Bonnie and Ruth, seated on steps.

14. (LtoR) Anita, Bonnie and Ruth, seated on steps.

15. (LtoR) Ruth, June and Anita at church, 1957.
Collection of the Authors.

16. Anita (seated in center, 4th from left,) Pre-Teen charm school at DeFremery
Recreation Center. Photo by E.F. Josephs / Courtesy Careth Reid.

FAIRYTALE

17. Ruth, Anita, Bonnie and June stand in driveway ready for church.

18. June.   19. Ruth with pocketbook.   20. Bonnie with pocketbook.

21. West Oakland Church of God Senior Choir, Elton Pointer, far right, Sarah Pointer 2nd row, second from right, Fritz, back row far right.

22. West Oakland Church of God Junior Choir. Paul Silas and Aaron Pointer (far left top row), Fritz Pointer (top row, 2nd from right,) standing next to Rose Gibson (far right,) Ruth (middle of 2nd row,) Anita (first row on right.) Collection of the Authors.

23. The 1965 Oakland Tech Drama program performing "The Skin of Our Teeth", (left to right) Anita in white shoes, Danny Mayfield, Ted Lange, Brenda Davis. Oakland Tech High School Yearbook.

24. Thomas Whayne, Drama teacher, Oakland Tech High School Yearbook.

25. Grandparents Roxie and Fritz Silas standing in front of their home on Green Lawn Street, Prescott, Arkansas.

26. Silas House on Green Lawn Street, Collection of the Authors.

27. The Negro Travelers' Green Book, guide for travel and vacations. Courtesy Digital Public Library of America.

28. The 1959 McClymonds (Mack) High School basketball team. Fritz #13 (standing 4th from left,) Aaron #10 (seated 3rd from right) and Paul Silas # 7 (seated 5th from right.) Collection of the Authors.

29. Ruth Pointer, Class of 1963.

30. Bonnie Pointer, Class of 1968.

31. Anita Pointer, Class of 1965.

32. Aaron Pointer (third from left) with other young men pose for
photographer in front of DeFremery Recreation Center.
Unknown photographer/Collection of the Author.

33. Paul Silas #35 "2-point hook shot" on court with Fritz #33,
Creighton University 1964 Yearbook.

34. (L-R) Fritz Pointer, Elton McGriff, "Chuck" Officer, Jim Bakus, Paul Silas, Bobby "Pops" Miles and Charlie Brown – the nationally ranked Creighton Blue Jays head to Miami, Florida, February 1964. Creighton University 1964 Yearbook.

35. Aaron Pointer Houston Astro's 1966 photo, Courtesy National Baseball Hall of Fame and Museum.

36. Elvin Bishop and band photographed at Keystone Korner, Anita on left front of frame, Bonnie on right, June seated back right. Photo by Bruce Steinberg.

37. June Pointer at sixteen.

38. Dave Mason with backup singers June, Anita and Bonnie Pointer. Composite photo from performance at Winterland, San Francisco, CA, April 28, 1972 Photo by Dan Cuny.

39. Rehearsing with Sylvester, Anita, Bonnie and Ruth, at Pepperland, December 31, 1971. Photo Clay Geerdes, Courtesy David Miller.

40. Dave Mason with backup singers Bonnie, June and Anita Pointer. Composite photo from performance photographed at Winterland, San Francisco, CA, April 28, 1972 by Dan Cuny.

41. Sylvester performing, June Bonnie and Anita back-up singers, San Francisco 1972.
Photo Clay Geerdes, Courtesy David Miller.

42. June, Photo Clay Geerdes,
Courtesy David Miller.

43. Bonnie, Photo Clay Geerdes,
Courtesy David Miller.

44. Anita, Photo Clay Geerdes,
Courtesy David Miller.

45. (LtoR) June, Bonnie (standing) and Anita. Photo by Herb Greene.

46. SAN FRANCISCO 1967: Concert promoter
Bill Graham poses for a portrait in 1967 in
San Francisco, California.
(Photo by Michael Ochs Archives/
Getty Images).

47. Herbie Hancock and David Rubinson.
Photo by Richard McCaffrey.

48. David Rubinson photographed at the newly opened recording studio
The Automatt. Photo by Richard McCaffrey.

49. Bonnie and Ruth 1973, Courtesy Norman Seeff.

50. Anita and June 1973, Courtesy Norman Seeff.

51. Jada seated next to table with sewing machine, BPP poster on back wall.
Rollingstone, 1971, Photo by Bruce Steinberg.

52. Roadside sign for the Lowndes County Freedom
Organization. The sign reads, "Pull the Lever for
the Black Panther and Go on Home!" Courtesy of
Jim Peppler Southern Courier photograph collection, Alabama Dept. of Archives and History.

53. Huey Newton and Fritz Pointer in front
of Merritt College after press conference.
With permission from The Dr. Huey P.
Newton Foundation, Courtesy of the
Department of Special Collections,
Stanford University Libraries.

54. Anita and Bonnie with bass player John Neumann captured at the
Troubadour show on July 13, 1973 by Sherry Rayn Barnett.

55. June at 20, 1974. Photographed by Herb Greene.

56. Bonnie at 24, 1974. Photographed by Herb Greene.

57. Anita at 26, 1974. Photographed by Herb Greene.

58. Ruth at 28, 1974. Photographed by Herb Greene.

59. Anita and Jada, with Mother Sarah's picture on the wall, photographed
at home by Moneta Sleet, Courtesy Johnson Publishing Company, LLC.
All rights reserved.

60. Anita, June, Jada, mother Sarah, Faun and Bonnie in kitchen at table laughing
at Malik's joke. Photographed at home by Moneta Sleet, Jr.,
Courtesy Johnson Publishing Company, LLC. All rights reserved.

61. The Pointer Sisters photographed in San Francisco by Moneta Sleet Jr.
Ebony Magazine, December 1973.

62. Back on the road, The Pointer Sisters waiting at the Philadelphia train station
(LtoR) with their road manager Linda Rogoff, June, Ruth, wardrobe mistress Linda Ryan,
Anita and Bonnie. Photographed by Moneta Sleet Jr.,

63. The marquee at Roseland Dance and the preshow excitement outside on West 52nd Street. The Pointer Sisters performance with Louis Jordan Tympany Five, one of the most popular bandleaders of the times, was a sold out not to be missed event. Photographed by Moneta Sleet Jr., Courtesy Johnson Publishing Company, LLC. All rights reserved.

64. Anita with Stevie Wonder backstage at Roseland. Collection of the Authors.

65. The Pointer Sisters (LtoR) Ruth, Bonnie, June and Anita, after the Berkeley concert are greeted backstage by their brother Fritz their father Rev. Elton Pointer and grandmother Mrs. Roxie Silas. Photographed by Moneta Sleet Jr., Courtesy Johnson Publishing Company, LLC. All rights reserved.

66. (Lto R) Unknown woman with arms around Faun, Anita with arms around Jada, Debbie Shine, Ruth, Michael Crowley, Bonnie and Daniel Mendez and June in the center. Photographed by Herb Greene.

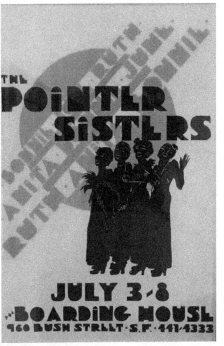

67. Poster from the Boarding House announcing the Pointer Sisters week of shows. Collection of the Authors.

68. Singing with Patty Andrews (center) on the TV special, One More Time in 1973. (LtoR: Ruth, Anita, Patty, Bonnie, June.) Courtesy Everett Collection.

69. The Pointer Sisters chat and have fun backstage in the Municipal Auditorium dressing room at the ABC/Dot Records show on Oct. 18, 1974. Blue Thumb didn't have a Country & Western (C&W) division, so Fairytale was promoted on the C&W market by ABC Dot Records, which like Blue Thumb, was part pf the Famous Music group. Photo: S.A. Tarkington / The Tennessean/ USA Today.

70. Fritz with Aaron home for a visit in Novato, CA.
Photo by Liziwe Kunene Pointer.

71. The Pointer Sisters performance at the Grand Ole Opry, the first Female African American singing group to appear at the famous venue, was captured by staff photographer Les Leverett in October of 1974. Image Courtesy of the Grand Ole Opry Archives.

72. The Pointer Sisters with Opry star Jeanne Pruett. Photo by Les Leverett. Image Courtesy of the Grand Ole Opry Archives.

73. Record executives Bob Krasnow and Gary Stromberg with David Rubinson holding the Pointer Sisters first gold record. Collection of the Authors.

74. June, Bonnie, Ruth and Anita pose with their first Grammy for Fairytale, 1975. Globe Photos/Zuma.

75. CAR WASH, (LtoR) Anita Pointer, June Pointer, Richard Pryor, Ruth Pointer,
Bonnie (Patricia) Pointer, 1976. Courtesy Everett Collection.

76. The Pointer Sisters appearing with Flip on the Flip Wilson Comedy Special,
(LtoR: Bonnie, Ruth, Anita and June) 1975. Courtesy Everett Collection.

77. The Pointer Sisters (LtoR: June, Anita, Bonnie and Ruth,) hold Carol Burnett's
arms on stage in a skit from the TV comedy series, 'The Carol Burnett Show,'
September 1975. Photo by CBS Photo Archive/Getty Images.

78. Anita, Ali and Bill Withers share lunch in Kinshasa, Zaire (now Democratic Republic of the Congo) during the 1974 Zaire Festival featuring a boxing match between George Foreman and Muhammad Ali promoted as The Rumble in the Jungle. Zaire 74 was a three-day live music festival that took place on September 22 to 24, 1974. Photo by Lynn Goldsmith.

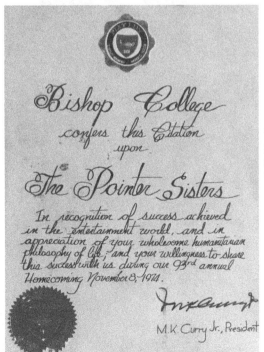

79. Bishop College Citation to the Pointer Sisters in recognition of success achieved, November 1974. Collection of the Authors.

80. Sarah Pointer (foreground) raises her grandchildren in Sausalito while the four singing Pointer Sisters are on tour in 1975. They are (from left behind couch) Jada Harper, 8, who is Anita Pointer's daughter and Malik Woods, 9, and his sister Faun. Next to their grandmother on the couch is her 83-year-old mother Roxie Silas and Mrs. Pointer's husband Elton, a retired minister. She is cuddling a little visitor Nandi Pointer, 3, her son Fritz's daughter. Photo by Alfred Arn/Marin Independent Journal.

81. Ruth, Anita, Bonnie and June with Don Cornelius on Soul Train.
Photo by Bruce Talamon.

82. Backstage at the Universal City Theater, 1976.
(Photo ©James Fortune, Rocket Pop Media).

83. Ruth, Anita and Bonnie joined their parents, Sarah and Elton Pointer, singing gospel during their week co-hosting with Mike Douglas. Their guests on this show also included the Happy Days cast, actors Ron Howard, Henry Winkler, Anson Williams and Donny Most and author Randall Schwartz. Collection of the Authors.

84. Anita on stage with the Pointer Sisters at the Roxy, Los Angeles 1977.
Bob Mackie designed these costumes for the Pointer Sisters.
Photo by Sherry Rayn Barnett.

85. The Pointer Sisters, performing in designer Bob Mackie 's one-shoulder blue metallic jumpsuits, featuring a feather plumed single right sleeve, and sequined keyboards from shoulder to ankle, down the right side. The outfits were originally worn performing an Elton John medley with Cher on "The Cher Show." They received the costumes later from Cher as a gift. (LtoR: June, Ruth, Anita and Bonnie.) Photo by Norman L. Hunter, Courtesy Johnson Publishing Company, LLC. All rights reserved.

86. Fritz with daughter Nandi, father Elton Pointer and brother Aaron, 1977 Photo by Liziwe Kunene Pointer.

87. Sarah and Elton Pointer in Hawaii. Collection of the Authors.

88. Having A Party, the Pointer Sisters 4th LP was recorded in and released in 1977. Although the record didn't chart well, it was a transitional record for the group; Bonnie would soon leave to pursue solo work and June would return. Photo by Michael Ochs Archives/Getty Images.

FAIRYTALE

89. Fritz Pointer and close friend David 'Mudavanha' Patterson, outside the former Pan African Cultural Center, aka the "Black House." Photo by Liziwe Kunene-Pointer.

90. Bonnie Pointer photographed during a private luncheon at the Johnson Publishing Company Chicago headquarters Photographed by Norman L. Hunter Courtesy Johnson Publishing Company, LLC. All rights reserved.

91. Sarah Pointer travelled to Europe with her daughters and was photographed in Milan. Collection of the Authors.

92. A rare photo of the six siblings (LtoR) Aaron, June, Bonnie, Anita, Ruth and Fritz. Photo by Liziwe Kunene Pointer, 1979.

93. Pointer Sisters with Merv Griffin holding Special Things, the first album without Bonnie. The record went Gold with the hit single He's So Shy. Courtesy Everett Collection.

94. Bonnie made the cover of Jet Magazine March 6th, 1980 telling readers "Freedom is Good, But Love is Better." Courtesy Johnson Publishing Company, LLC. All rights reserved.

95. Fritz and James Baldwin were photographed when Baldwin visited and spoke at Luther College, Decorah, Iowa. Photo by Liziwe Kunene-Pointer.

97. June with Richard Perry in the studio. Collection of the Authors.

96. The Pointer Sisters on the cover of Jet Magazine, 1980, announcing they've "Shed Old Look, Clothes, Reach New Heights." Courtesy Johnson Publishing Company.

98. The Decade Twins, Fritz and June taken at Fritz' home in 1979. Collection of the Authors.

99. Fritz and wife, Liziwe Kunene-Pointer at Luther College, Decorah, Iowa. Fritz was featured in the Des Moines paper for his success as Professor with the African Studies program at the school. Courtesy of Luther College Archives.

100. The Pointer Sisters, " So Excited" photographed in 1982. Courtesy Norman Seeff.

101. Pointer Sisters, (L-R, June, Anita, and Ruth,) hold two American Music Awards for Favorite Black Group and Favorite Black Video Group for their music video Dare Me. The 12th Annual American Music Awards were held on January 28, 1985 at the Shrine Auditorium in Los Angeles. Los Angeles Herald Examiner Photo Collection.

102. Contact, their 11th studio album was released in 1985, was certified Platinum. Photo by Richard E. Aaron/Redferns/Getty.

103. "We Are The World" is a charity single originally recorded by the super group
United Support of Artists (USA) for Africa in 1985. It was written by Michael Jackson
and Lionel Richie and produced by Quincy Jones for the album We Are The World.
The song was released on March 7, 1985, as the first single from the album.
The first ever single to be certified multi-platinum, it received a Quadruple Platinum
certification, three Grammy's, one American Music Award and a People's Choice
Award. Courtesy The Everett Collection.

104. Pointer Sisters, L-R, June, Anita, and Ruth and Bruce Willis teamed up in a rockin' musical TV Special The Pointer Sisters Up All Night. On the Special, The Pointer Sisters accompanied Willis and performed original songs from his upcoming debut album. 1987 NBC promotional hand out.

105. Backstage after the show in Las Vegas (LtoR) June, Diahann Carroll, Ruth, Julie Belafonte, Anita, Sammy Davis Jr. and Harry Belafonte. Collection of the Authors.

106. The cast of Ain't Misbehavin' in Bob Mackie costumes, 1995.
Courtesy of The Everett Collection.

107. Anita in the studio, recording the soundtrack of Ain't Misbehavin', 1995. Photo by Joan Marcus.

108. Anita with Sandy Gallin, 1987 (Sandy Gallin, 1940-2017) Collection of the Authors.

109. June, Anita and Ruth with Clint Black, 1994. Photo by Afro American Newspapers/Gado/Getty Images.

110. June, Anita and Ruth sang the National Anthem during an NFL game between the Cincinnati Bengals and the Los Angeles Raiders where brother Aaron was a referee. Nov. 5, 1989 in Los Angeles. Collection of the Authors.

111. A Party for the Greatest, Muhammad Ali's 50th Birthday celebration
broadcast that took place at the Wiltern Theater, February of 1992.
Courtesy George Schlatter Productions.

112. Anita, President Bill Clinton, Ruth, Hillary Clinton and June 1994.
Collection of the Authors.

113. Ruth, Bonnie, June and Anita were honored with a Hollywood Star ceremony marking
their 20th anniversary in the music business. Sept 29, 1994. Collection of the Authors.

114. June with Joann, 1995. Photo by
Liziwe Kunene Pointer.

115. Fritz and Noor Ebrahim (curator of the District Six Museum, Cape Town,
South Africa), exchanging books. Photo by Liziwe Kunene-Pointer.

116. Anita Pointer's Oakland White Sox Little League team.

117. Anita received The Oakland Babe
Ruth League 1993 City Tournament,
1st Place Sponsor trophy.

118. Jada and Anita.

119. Fritz and wife Liziwe Kunene Pointer, in Monaco 2010,
Collection of the Authors.

120. Fritz visiting backstage at Berkeley's Zellerbach Hall, with Hugh Masekela and
Danny Glover. Photo by Liziwe Kunene-Pointer.

121. Anita with daughter Jada and baby Roxie, 1991. Craig Skinner/Globe Photos.

122. Anita Jada and June.

123. Jada, Anita, Baby Roxie and Mother Sarah.

124. Jada with daughter Roxie, 1998. Collection of the Authors.

125. Aaron at a meeting of The Black Collective in Tacoma, Washington - 2010.

126. Anita, a strong Queen of her castle, poses with a tiny gold crown and a healthy sense of humor, after battling Uterine cancer in 2011. Photo by Liziwe Kunene-Pointer.

127. Fritz Pointer with the Pointer Sister's display at the Smithsonian National Museum of African American History and Culture in Washington, D.C. October 8, 2016. Photo by Liziwe Kunene-Pointer.

128. Some of the many amazing awards and recognitions that Anita and her sisters have collected over the years.

129. Anita at her home in Beverly Hills with some of her historical African American Black Memorabilia collection. Collection of the Authors.

130. Bonnie, Stevie Wonder and Anita at funeral services for
Andrae Crouch, 2016. Collection of the Authors.

131. Anita and Bonnie attend the 3rd Roger Neal Style Hollywood (RNSH) Oscar Viewing
Black Tie Dinner Gala Presented by Suzan Hughes Education Foundation S.H.E. Photo by
Clinton H.Wallace/Photomundo International/Globe Photos Inc.

132. Our mother, Sarah Pointer. Collection of the Authors.

133. Our father, Elton Pointer. Collection of the Authors.

INDEX

CPSIA information can be obtained
at www.ICGtesting.com
Printed in the USA
BVHW072240300120
571050BV00002B/4

9 781948 018388